"... a comprehensive, easy-to-follow guide ..."
—Bill Colson, *Sports Illustrated*

"Must reading for parents of beginning players"
—Donna Fales, Past-President, National Junior Tennis League

"... concise, easy to understand ..."
—Jim Martz, *Miami Herald*

"Parents familiar with tennis as well as those new to the sport will find value in this guide."
—Robert Langram, Villanova University

"... a comprehensive teaching guide for beginners."
—Layton Charles, *Fort Meyers News Press*

"... Gives parents useful guidelines for starting children off."
—Rick Mewhirter, *Boca Raton News*

A PARENT'S GUIDE TO
COACHING TENNIS

A PARENT'S GUIDE TO

COACHING TENNIS

Pierce Kelley

BETTERWAY BOOKS
CINCINNATI, OHIO

The Parent's Guide to Coaching Tennis. Copyright © 1995 by Pierce Kelley. Printed and bound in the United States of America. All rights reserved. No part of this book may be reproduced in any form or by any electronic or mechanical means including information storage and retrieval systems without permission in writing from the publisher, except by a reviewer, who may quote brief passages in a review. Published by Betterway Books, an imprint of F&W Publications, Inc., 1507 Dana Avenue, Cincinnati, Ohio 45207. 1-800-289-0963. First edition.

99   98   97   96   95   5   4   3   2   1

Library of Congress Cataloging-in-Publication Data

Kelley, Pierce
   The parent's guide to coaching tennis / Pierce Kelley. — Rev. ed.
     p.   cm.
   Includes bibliographical references and index.
   ISBN 1-55870-369-1
   1. Tennis for children—Coaching. I. Title.
GV1001.4.C45K45   1995
796.342′083—dc20   95-5540
                                                     CIP

Edited by Diana Martin
Cover and Interior design by Sandy Conopeotis Kent

ACKNOWLEDGMENTS

There are a number of people I would like to recognize for their assistance and support of this project. First and foremost, I thank my wife and children for providing me with the insight and perspective necessary to write this book. Although Von Beebe did a terrific job taking virtually all of the photographs, his most valuable contribution was his encouragement throughout the tedious and time-consuming revisions, for which I thank him.

I acknowledge and thank Gerry McGuffin, formerly of the USTA's Education and Research Office in Princeton, New Jersey, for her invaluable suggestions and assistance. Chuck Levitt of the Little Professor Bookstore in Omaha, Nebraska, provided me with advice and counsel, for which I am grateful. I also wish to thank my typist, Teresa Fernandez, as well as the many friends who reviewed the various drafts for me.

I am most grateful, also, to Jimmy and Colette Evert for their contribution to this book. I have no doubt but that their support of this book gives it added credibility to readers. As a token of my appreciation, a portion of any moneys I realize from the sale of this book will be donated to the Evert Family College Scholarship Fund, which is administered by the Youth Tennis Foundation of Florida and which rewards deserving high school seniors for good sportsmanship.

Finally, I wish to thank Mert Ransdell of F&W Publications, Inc. for her confidence in my book and her willingness and enthusiasm toward the revised edition. I also thank Diana Martin for her contribution to and improvement of the book.

ABOUT THE AUTHOR

Pierce Kelley, a nationally ranked player in 1970, is the director and host of a PBS television show on introducing children to tennis. He is an attorney, president of the Youth Tennis Foundation of Florida and a member of the U.S. Professional Tennis Association, and has been involved in youth tennis programs since 1971. He lives with his wife, Christine, and their four children in Tarpon Springs, Florida.

To all those who helped me learn what I have learned from and about the game of tennis, most particularly my parents; and to all those I have helped or tried to help along the way, especially the children, whose shared enjoyment of the game makes it all worthwhile, most particularly my children.

FOREWORD
by Jimmy Evert

My wife Colette and I have been blessed with five healthy children who, much to our delight, have all become excellent tennis players. All of us worked very hard for that to happen. At first, our hope was that they would enjoy playing tennis and become good club players who would benefit from the social aspects of the game. I have been a teaching professional for more than thirty-five years and was able to provide the necessary instruction. That was only half the job. Colette and I devoted much time and attention to nurturing their interest in the game, so that they would enjoy playing tennis and not simply do as we asked them to do.

Most parents do not have the years of playing and teaching experience that I have, and they need the assistance of a qualified teaching pro. The choice of a qualified tennis professional is only half the job. Few, if any, young children become good tennis players, let alone great ones, without the support and encouragement of their parents. Pierce Kelley has written a book that will be useful to all parents of aspiring tennis players. It will be especially helpful for those of you who either have not played tennis at all, or have not played very much tennis. However, it will be of much benefit to knowledgeable tennis-playing parents as well.

Colette and I have known Pierce Kelley, his parents, brothers and sister since he was one of the top junior players in the state of Florida almost thirty years ago. In recent years Pierce has been active with an organization known as the Youth Tennis Foundation of Florida, which has helped thousands of young players around the state through a team tennis program for unranked tennis players, by providing a college scholarship service to graduating high school players, and by awarding scholarships to deserving players who have exhibited good sportsmanship and conduct, among other worthwhile activities. We know Pierce to be a fine tennis player who enjoys sharing his knowledge of the game with others, particularly young children. When he asked me to write the foreword to his book after reviewing it, I was more than happy to assist him.

I am often asked by parents of the children I teach what they can do to participate in the learning process. Invariably I tell them to practice with their children between lessons. I give them various exercises and drills to use in their practice sessions, but I have never had any written materials to give them. Pierce's book will help me teach beginning children, because if parents read his book and follow his suggestions, we will all benefit.

This book tells you, as parents, how to do the other half of the job. The emphasis on making playing tennis fun is terrific. Maintaining the proper perspective is excellent advice. The drills and games are very practical and easy to follow. In sum, I wholeheartedly recommend this book to parents of beginning players and wish good luck to all of you who want your children to become tennis players. Not all children will become champions, but tennis can provide a lifetime of family entertainment and togetherness. This book will increase your chances of successfully introducing your children to the game of tennis.

INTRODUCTION

INTRODUCTION

Although tennis is now being taught, along with other sports, in some public schools and at recreation departments, most children begin to learn how to play tennis from their parents. If a child shows interest, lessons from a tennis professional will be arranged. If the initial experience is not an enjoyable one, it is very easy for a child to become frustrated, lose interest, and find something else to do. This book provides a guide for you to successfully introduce your child to the game of tennis. The key ingredient is to make the time you spend together on and around a tennis court enjoyable for both you and your child.

The parent who reads this book does not have to be a knowledgeable player. In fact, it will be most useful for parents with little or no knowledge of the game. It tells how you can spend time with your child on a tennis court practicing what your child has been taught from teaching professionals. Nontennis-playing parents can learn about tennis and grow with their children in the process. If your child practices between lessons, his performance will improve at future lessons. If the practice sessions are done well, the likelihood that your child will want to continue taking lessons will dramatically increase.

Also, and most important, this book tells you how to become your child's first "tennis coach" even if you don't have the knowledge or expertise of a teaching professional. Parents are a child's primary authority figures. Just as success in school is directly related to parental support of classroom activities, success in athletics, whether it be tennis or any other sport, requires the same degree of support by parents. However, most parents, even those who are knowledgeable players, are often uncertain as to what they can or should do. All parents should establish themselves as their child's first "coach" even though there is a tennis pro providing the instruction. You need to have a good idea as to what your child should and should not be doing. You don't need to be an expert, but you need to be able to identify easily recognizable mistakes.

I have taught tennis to children of all ages, backgrounds and abilities at public playgrounds and country clubs, in both rural and metropolitan areas. I sincerely believe that I learned more about teaching tennis to children when I began to teach my own children to play than at any other time. I wrote this book to share with other parents what I have learned through the years.

I find it useful to compare the process of teaching a child to play tennis to that of teaching a child to play catch. Most parents think of playing catch with their child as fun, quality time, even though it takes years to master throwing and catching a baseball or football. It will help if you can keep that same frame of mind when practicing tennis with your child. Most children think and plan only in terms of days and weeks. Their goal is to enjoy themselves. They won't be concerned about slow progress. Hence, you are the one who must be patient and try to make certain that your child is learning correctly and is having fun in the process. It will, however, require more than patience and a positive frame of mind to teach your child to play tennis.

More than anything else, this book tells you how to make learning to play tennis fun. I have included a chapter and much discussion with regard to the technical aspects of the game, but the main thrust of the book is to let you know how to make the experience an enjoyable one for your child. If your child is happy, that should make you happy, too. If you believe that the time and effort required for your child to learn to play tennis are worthwhile, you just might find that tennis can be a new, fun activity to share with your child for a lifetime.

Chapter One

A BRIEF HISTORY OF TENNIS

Although it is hardly necessary for you or your child to know the history of tennis to learn how to play, you may be curious about it. After all, children are taught that James Naismith invented the game of basketball from his Springfield, Massachusetts, home and that Alexander Cartwright of New York invented the game of baseball. Who invented the game of tennis and when?

Englishman Major Walter Clopton Wingfield is credited as the inventor of tennis, although the game has changed quite a bit since he designed and patented it in 1874. His original version involved an hourglass-shaped court and a fifteen-point scoring system. It was called *sphairistike*, a Greek word meaning "playing at ball." Shortly after Major Wingfield created the game, the All-England Croquet Club, located in the London suburb of Wimbledon, actually developed the game into what it is now. After a single tennis court was added to the grounds around 1876, club members showed immediate interest. The club added more courts and changed its name to the All-England Croquet Club and Lawn Tennis Club. The first Wimbledon championships were held in 1877. The sport has been growing bigger and better ever since.

While tennis is a sport in which a racket and a ball are used as in baseball, cricket, lacrosse, squash, jai alai and other sports, its evolution is traced to a thirteenth-century French game *jeu de paume* or "game of the palm" that used the hands and a spherical ball. At first only the nobility were able to play the game, which was passed on from the French gentility to their English counterparts. After the French Revolution, the game was abolished in France, and England carried on the tradition.

Dr. James Dwight of New York is credited with being the father of American tennis. In 1881 he created the United States Lawn Tennis Association in which tennis-playing enthusiasts in the United States, who were primarily located in the northeast, could participate. The first men's national championship tournament was held at the Newport Casino in Newport, Rhode Island, in 1881. The first women's national championship took place in 1887.

The tournament was moved to the West Side Tennis Club in Forest Hills, New York, in 1915 and then, for one year, to the Germantown Cricket Club in Philadelphia, prior to returning to Forest Hills. The national championships, now known as the U.S. Open, moved to the present site at Flushing Meadow, New York, in 1978.

The national tournament is called the U.S. Open because it is "open" to all, professionals and amateurs. Until 1968, professionals were not allowed to compete with nonprofessionals, and professionals were not permitted to play in any of the major tournaments. It took almost forty years of "barnstorming" and other commercial efforts by many of the game's most prominent heroes before the game of tennis became more like other sports, wherein the best players in the world compete against each other and anyone else for compensation and recognition as the greatest players in the world. Some of the pioneers of professional tennis were Bill Tilden, Suzanne Lenglen, Ellsworth Vines, Fred Perry, Don Budge, Bobby Riggs, Jack Kramer, Pancho Gonzales, Lew Hoad, Ken Rosewall and Rod Laver.

Many of the major tennis tournaments in the world were played on grass courts until the mid-1970s when the United States determined that clay courts were a better surface for the national championships, since they were more abundant than grass courts. The "lawn" was dropped from the United States Lawn Tennis Association's name and the U.S. Open was first played on a clay court in 1975. In 1978, the tournament was moved to Flushing Meadow, where the court surface is an asphalt-based or "hard" surface. Most of the other grass court tournaments were dropped from the tournament circuit as well, although Wimbledon is still played on grass and remains the premier tournament in the world.

Very few tournaments are now played on grass courts in the United States. The most prominent grass court tournament remaining is, most appropriately, a Hall of Fame tournament held annually in Newport, Rhode Island, in August. The Newport Casino houses the International Tennis Hall of Fame and Tennis Museum. New enshrinees are annually inducted into the Hall of Fame while the tournament is being played, much like the NFL and NBA Hall of Fame games.

Should your youngster inquire, you can surprise your child with some of this historical information.

References

Wingfield: Edwardian Gentleman, by George E. Alexander (Peter E. Randall, 1986)

Official Yearbook, United States Tennis Association (1990)

Training Manual, United States Professional Tennis Association

Chapter Two

THE FIRST STEPS

The best age to begin teaching your child to play tennis is when he is six or seven, even though, at first, he may lack the physical strength to handle the racket correctly. Children younger than six lack the necessary attention span and simply don't have enough size or strength to make your time and effort worthwhile. Tossing balls to a young child for him to catch or hit undoubtedly helps to develop his eye-hand coordination and is therefore worthwhile, but the time spent should be considered as fun, quality time, rather than a serious attempt to begin the instruction of tennis.

Some people, however, do think it is productive to begin as early as age three by revising the game to suit the size of the child. One racket manufacturer is offering for three-year-olds a line of rackets with Disney characters on them. Another has a program for four-year-olds that simply reduces the sizes of the court and racket and lowers the net, among other changes. This book presupposes that the instruction begins at six years of age.

No matter at what age your child begins, I suggest that he or she begin with a small group of friends. If you can assemble two or three other reasonably manageable, motivated children who wish to take lessons together, you will be off to a good start. There are also financial benefits in doing so, as most tennis pros charge for their time and not by the number of children on the court. Also, if and when your child decides that tennis is fun and he wants to continue playing, he will need friends to play with. I believe you will find that your child's interest in taking lessons or in practicing with you will be greatly increased if his friends are there.

EQUIPMENT YOU WILL NEED

When you take that first step toward having your child receive instruction, you don't need to spend any money on new clothes or

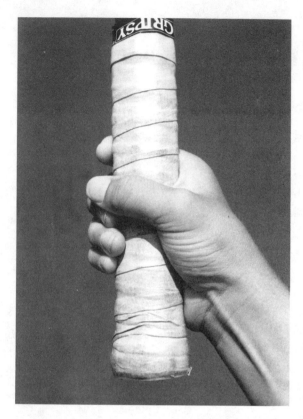

To correctly grip a racket, the tip of your child's thumb should meet the first joint of his middle finger, with the hand spread out loosely around the racket.

new sneakers. Your child will be much more comfortable and relaxed wearing the shorts, T-shirts and sneakers he or she is used to. The only equipment you will need to buy is a racket and some balls to practice with.

Racket

Unless your child is a teenager or has large hands, you should buy a junior racket. The things to consider when purchasing a racket, in addition to the cost, are the size of the grip, the length of the racket, and the size of the racket "face" (the stringed portion of the racket). There is an enormous assortment of rackets from which to choose for young children. Junior rackets of several manufacturers are described in Appendix E.

Junior rackets come in varying grip sizes from 3½″ to 4⅛″ in circumference. Be sure that the child can get his hand around the racket easily, and that he uses the proper grip, shown on page 6.

There are three basic racket face sizes from which to choose: standard, midsize and oversized. An oversized racket face is approximately 110 square inches or larger. A midsize is usually 90 to 95 square inches. Anything less is in the standard category. There is a difference of opinion among professionals as to which is best. The larger racket face gives children a larger hitting area and, therefore, a much better chance of making contact with the ball. Success in hitting the ball will boost your child's self-confidence and make it more likely that he will enjoy the experience. It is no fun for him to swing and miss, no matter how much reassurance you offer. If your child is strong enough to handle the oversized racket, it may be the best way to go. If the oversized racket is too heavy or too unwieldy, begin with a smaller racket. I recommend the midsize racket, as I find the hitting area large enough and the racket more easily handled.

Children's rackets come in varying lengths of 21 to 26 inches. (A racket that is 27 inches long is the full, adult size.) The appropriate length of the racket depends on how tall and how strong your child is. Resist the urge to begin with an old racquetball racket. Choose the longest racket your child is comfortable with. The racket should be at least as long as your child's arm.

An adequate racket can be purchased for less than twenty dollars. A top-quality junior racket can be bought for less than seventy-five dollars. The difference in price is largely a matter of what the racket is made of. You can still buy wooden rackets, which are the cheapest. There are also aluminum, steel alloy, graphite and composition rackets. Nowadays most are composed of several materials. For the racket face, inexpensive nylon, strung at 50 to 55 pounds of tension, is adequate. If you need help in choosing a racket, ask the pro who will be teaching your child for assistance.

Balls

A new can of balls costs two to three dollars. However, if you can get enough used balls from your tennis-playing friends, you can

The ball hopper picks up and holds
practice balls, saving time and exertion
for you and your child.

Coaching Tennis

save yourself some money. It is best to have a large number of balls to work with so you can keep tossing the balls as quickly as possible in order to hold your child's interest. If you spend most of the time picking up balls, it will be hard for you to generate as much enthusiasm as you would like. Also, to reduce the frustration of bending over to pick up balls throughout the sessions, you may want to invest in a "ball hopper," which picks up and holds the practice balls. These come in different sizes. The middle size holds approximately seventy-five balls and costs about thirty dollars.

Optional Equipment

A wide variety of clothing and accessories are available that can enhance your child's enjoyment of playing tennis. Whether it is the bright, colorful Andre Agassi look or traditional whites, it is important for some children to feel good about how they look on the court and the equipment that they have. For some, if they like their racket, clothing and equipment, they will enjoy playing more. Here are a number of inexpensive ways to make that happen, since you could also spend a lot of money if you don't watch out.

Rackets come in different sizes, shapes and colors. You can buy a racket unstrung and have a pattern of different colored strings put in it. Some rackets come with different colored strings already in them. You can also have the strings painted in any figure or letter you wish. Grips also come in different colors. There is gauze in a variety of colors to put around the grip. There are colorful protective devices or materials that you can put over the top of the racket to protect it from scraping the ground.

There are headbands, wristlets and socks for your selection, and a nearly limitless variety of shorts, T-shirts, tennis dresses, warm-up outfits, hats, shoes and other clothing.

There are many gadgets and other items of interest to children. One is a foam spongelike piece that is placed on the strings of the racket and is said to reduce the vibration. While this may be helpful for older players who are worried about tennis elbow, I am certain that for children it is merely the aesthetic quality that is important. Ball holders can be worn by a small child who is unable to hold two balls at the same time. Athletic bags and towels and other accessories abound. Even tennis balls come in different colors.

While this optional equipment is, without doubt, relatively inconsequential, these extras may well be the proverbial "carrot," to get your child moving in the right direction.

CHOOSING A TENNIS PROFESSIONAL

Choosing a tennis professional is an important decision, so be a wise consumer. Tennis professionals are not all the same. Some are better players than teachers and vice versa. Each one teaches differently. Some charge more than others, but this does not necessarily mean that the more expensive pro is better. Some tennis pros are members of the United States Professional Tennis Association, Inc. (USPTA), but this does not mean that he or she is superior to a pro who is not a member. To become USPTA members pros must pass both written and performance tests that gauge their knowledge of the game and their ability to play and teach the game. Also, the USPTA provides continuing education programs for its members as well as umbrella liability insurance coverage and other benefits that could be of value to you. Some pros are members of the United States Professional Tennis Registry (USPTR), which is another worthwhile organization and has similar requirements and advantages. I recommend that you shop around.

In addition to the cost of lessons, ask if the cost varies if one child is taught as opposed to four children and, if so, by how much. The pro's fee should be the same regardless of the number of children involved in a lesson. Find out if the pro or his assistant will be giving the lessons. Find out about the junior programs the pro has developed and the number of junior players at the courts. Proximity of the courts to your child's home or school is certainly a factor to be considered as well.

You and your child should meet the prospective pro before engaging his or her services, since it is most important for both of you to be comfortable with him. I suggest you watch the pro give a lesson to children and see how he or she acts toward and talks to the children. If the children seem to like the pro and to be interested in the lesson, the chances of your child's success will be greatly increased. You should also look at issues such as junior programs, the pro's USPTA membership, his playing experience (i.e., past or present ranking) and word-of-mouth recommendations.

Every pro teaches differently and has different opinions on tennis technique, such as how to hold the racket and hit the ball. It is extremely important that your child learn the fundamentals of the game correctly in the beginning stages. It is, therefore, important to choose a quality tennis professional, and you should rely on that professional for the fine details of tennis instruction.

ESTABLISHING YOURSELF AS COACH

A child receives coaching, usually not from parents, in almost every other organized sport that he or she participates in, such as football, basketball, baseball or soccer. And, since tennis, until very recently, was not played as a team sport with a coach until a player reached high school, a youngster did not receive any coaching until he had already become an experienced, advanced player. The tennis pro can provide the instruction during a lesson, but frequent lessons can become expensive. For every hour of lessons, your child should practice at least three hours. As your child improves, the practice time should increase. During practice sessions, you should establish a relationship with your child which is just like that of coach.

Your role as coach involves more than simply being a practice partner or providing moral support. You must shape your child's character and personality on and around a tennis court. Tennis, as a sport, has been subjected to much scrutiny as to why so many of its top players are temperamental and exhibit tantrums and other examples of poor behavior. The first explanation is that tennis is an individual sport and there is, necessarily, more pressure on the tennis player than there is on any one member of a team. Others say that athletes are all high-strung competitors who react similarly, and that the crowd usually doesn't hear the outbursts of baseball or football players, since they are made either to the umpires or referees or occur when the players return to the bench after something upsets them. In tennis, a player is said to be under a microscope. Regardless of the causes or the explanations, no parent wants to see his child behave in such a way as to embarrass himself or his family.

Ultimately, it is you who must teach your child how to behave in the heat of battle. However, you can't be too domineering, as this also will cause problems. I'm sure you have a horror story or two to tell of a particular parent who repeatedly made a spectacle of himself at an athletic event by being too boisterous and enthusiastic in support of his child. Such parents are usually unduly harsh in their criticisms of their child or the coach or a referee, yet are just as excited in their praise of a winning performance. They simply want the best for their child and fail to see themselves as others do.

The answer lies in the approach you take to the entire process of playing tennis. While it is a tired cliché, tennis is just a game, as is any other sport, and if your child truly does not like to play tennis, for whatever reasons, don't push him into playing, because then tennis will not be fun and won't be just a game. There are so many worthwhile activities to interest a child, it really shouldn't matter what activity your child chooses to pursue, provided it is a wholesome and healthy activity. If your child isn't interested in anything, a little forceful persuasion may be necessary.

As a parent, you should begin by realizing that, despite your best efforts, your child may not like to play tennis. Approach the sport with the attitude that you and your child will "try" tennis to see if the child likes it. You should not have many behavior problems in the beginning stages with that perspective. The problem will come if your child develops an interest in the game and becomes frustrated if he does not do as well as he would like.

At this stage, tennis is not the most important activity in a child's life, nor is any other sport. Don't make tennis too important during the early years. Some children are put under pressure very early on, usually with poor results. A friend of mine, who is a teaching tennis professional, related a story of an extremely talented ten-year-old who had temper tantrums and threw his racket and shouted obscenities if things did not go his way. His parents took his rackets away for a year and refused to allow him to play. The parents established their authority and put tennis in proper perspective. A few years later, the child was among the best players in the country in his age group and was not exhibiting any more tantrums.

If a child has talent, he or she will ultimately be successful, even if the child does not pursue the activity exclusively during the formative years. The United States Tennis Association has recently eliminated a national championship for the twelve-and-under category in order to reduce competition and thereby reduce the prospect of "burnout" for the very young. I suggest to you that if you keep tennis in the proper perspective, family and school will be seen as the top priorities, and your child's perspective is less likely to be skewed.

Having said all of that, let's return to the question of your role as coach. In tennis, which is not unlike other sports on this issue, your child will hear many things from many people as to how a ball should be hit or the best way to grip a racket. Eventually, at a much later stage, your child will have to decide for himself who to listen to and what direction to follow. At the outset, both you and your child should be willing to follow the instructions given by the chosen professional and to go along with the program. In the beginning stages, there should be no disagreement between you and the information your child is receiving from any other source. Even though you do not have as much technical knowledge or skill as the tennis professional, you are still the primary authority figure.

Practice sessions between you and your child (and a few of the child's friends) should be a time for practicing what the pro has taught. You need to know what your child was taught. Ask questions of the pro to make certain you conduct the practice sessions properly. The tennis pro is the instructor, and you are the "coach" of the practice sessions. Consider wearing a coach's hat or shirt or carry a whistle to help establish the relationship. A strong parent/child "coaching" relationship will do more than anything else to prevent your child from behaving in an offensive and embarrassing way on the court. If you think of yourself as a coach, it is more likely that your child will too. So, think of yourself as the coach, maintain the proper perspective, and enjoy yourself and your child.

Chapter Three

WHAT TO TEACH BEFORE THE FIRST LESSON

There are a number of things for your child to learn before he walks onto a tennis court for the first time. You can teach your child (and his friends) some of these things in preparation for the first session and save the pro the trouble of spending time doing so.

THIRTEEN RULES OF TENNIS ETIQUETTE

Good behavior on and around a tennis court is not something that will come naturally. Tennis is a different activity from soccer or football since at a tennis match, whether amateur or pro, silence from the spectators is the rule. At other sports events the more noise the crowd makes the better. It is important that your child recognize this difference from the start, although this is not as important when the child is taking a lesson, since the pro will control the situation. But it may be extremely important when you go off on your own to practice. You can reinforce these rules by pointing out to your child how players and spectators behave during a match.

- Do not scream or talk loudly while on or around the courts.
- Do not throw your racket or ball.
- Try to stop your balls before they roll onto another court.
- Never walk on another court while a point is in progress.
- Always walk behind a court, as close to the back fence as possible, when walking across a court in use.
- Always return a ball that comes onto your court from another court as soon as possible.
- Always retrieve your balls from someone else's court without their assistance, if you can do so without interrupting their game.

- Do not sit on, or lean against the net or hit it with your racket.
- If other people are waiting to play, let them know how long you have been playing and how much longer you will be on the court.
- Dress appropriately, which is determined by the manner of dress at or guidelines of a particular tennis facility.
- Before your first session at a tennis center, inquire about the "off hours" for serious or regular players. Find out which days of the week and what time periods would be best for you. Some centers may have rules limiting the number of players on a court or the number of balls you can use.
- Try to reserve a court for practice that is isolated from other courts or fenced in as much as possible.
- If you cannot find an isolated court, it is a good idea to ask neighboring players for their patience before starting your practice sessions.

THE LINES OF THE COURT

Next, teach your child about the court lines so he will begin to understand that there are certain areas for hitting or serving the ball. Use the diagrams on the opposite page to teach and to test about the lines. Your child will be doing well if he can remember base line, service line and net.

THE PARTS OF THE RACKET

Show your child the various parts of the racket, first using the diagram on page 18, and then testing his knowledge using his own racket. This information, particularly the difference between the racket head and face, will help your child understand a pro's instruction about grip and hitting.

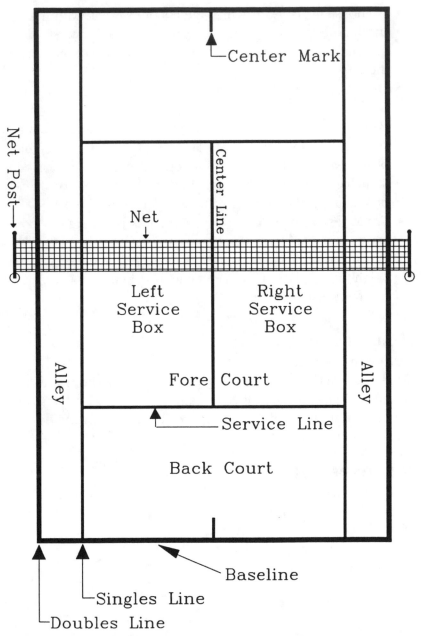

Each line and section of the court has a name, sometimes more than one. Players and pros will refer to the lines or sections by name; your child should memorize them as quickly as possible.

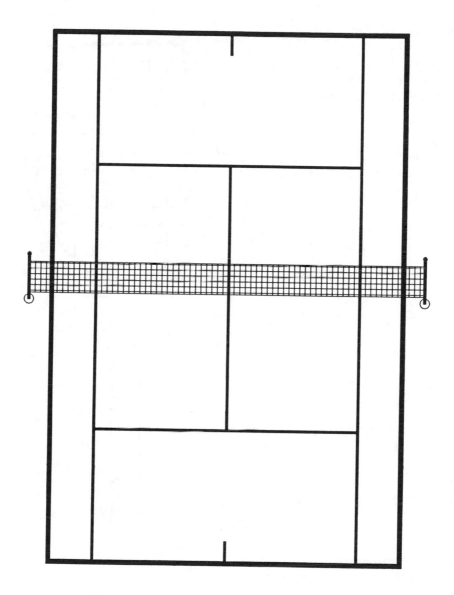

Use this court diagram to test your child's memory of the names of the court lines.

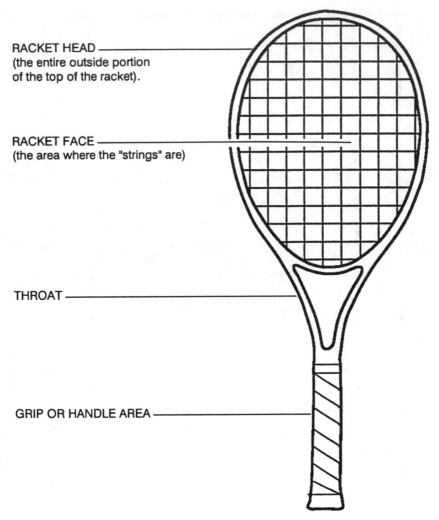

RACKET HEAD
(the entire outside portion
of the top of the racket).

RACKET FACE
(the area where the "strings" are)

THROAT

GRIP OR HANDLE AREA

Help your child memorize the parts of
the racket, then test his knowledge
using the diagram on the next page.

1. ————————————————
(the entire outside portion
of the top of the racket).

2. ————————————————

3. ————————————————

4. ————————————————

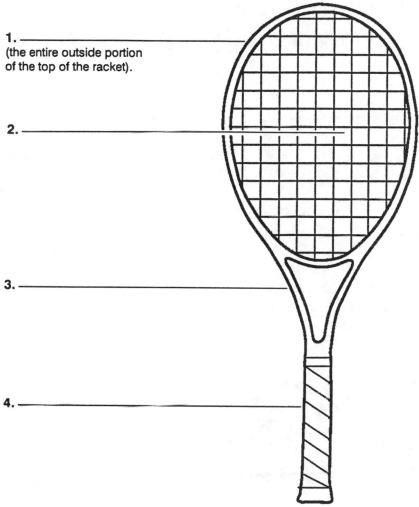

Use this diagram to test your child's
knowledge of the parts of the racket.

Chapter Four

HOW TO HIT THE BALL

This section will give you some insight into what the professional is teaching, with minor variations, so that you will have a better understanding of how your child should stand, hold the racket, swing the racket and hit the ball.

HOW TO STAND ON THE COURT

In tennis, as in most other sports, a player does not know where the ball will be hit by the opponent and must be ready for whatever shot is hit and the way it bounces. How your child stands when expecting to hit a ball is called the *ready position* or *stance*. The correct ready position is shown in the photo below. The photos on the opposite page show common problems to watch for and correct.

The correct stance includes feet spread a shoulder width apart and placed the same distance from the net; knees slightly bent; racket pointed at the opponent, with the racket head raised slightly and at chest level; and the child's weight forward on the balls of the feet, not on the heels.

STANCE TROUBLESHOOTING

Here the feet are too close together and the knees are rigid, causing an erect stance.

The racket needs to be at chest level, the knees need to bend, and the child's weight needs to move forward onto the balls of her feet.

HOW TO HOLD THE RACKET

The single most important thing for your child to learn is how to hold the racket. The way a player holds the racket is called the *grip*. Once your child learns an incorrect or an unorthodox grip and plays and practices with that grip, it is extremely difficult to change. What will surprise a new initiate to tennis is the impact of making even a ⅛-inch shift in racket position. A trained eye can easily tell what grip a child is using by how he or she swings the racket. Later, as the player develops, it makes a difference in how the game is played.

Virtually all acceptable grips fall into three basic categories: eastern, continental and western. The western grip is subdivided into a full western and a semiwestern; these are shown on page 26. Because great players have used any one of these grips, few teaching professionals will say that one grip is right and another wrong. I recommend the continental grip because (among other reasons) it is the easiest for your child to learn. The main reason I recommend the continental is that, unlike the other grips, a child can hit all shots without having to change the placement of his or her hands on the racket. If desired, a child can change from a continental to an eastern in a year or two without much difficulty. Jimmy Evert feels quite strongly that the eastern is the best grip to teach a beginner, which is the orthodox view. Others say the semiwestern grip is the best because many of the top players in the game today are using that grip. A few top players use a full western, although it is seldom recommended by a teaching pro. There are several grips that no one defends and are simply wrong, such as putting a thumb behind the racket grip to hit a backhand or a finger behind the grip to hit a forehand, which many beginners, adults as well as children, do because they lack strength in their wrist. Another example is putting a thumb on top of the grip, much as one might grip a Ping-Pong paddle. What makes such grips wrong is that they have proved to be ineffective and inadequate at higher levels of play. Beginners may "get by" with using such grips, but they will not advance past the beginning or intermediate stage with such grips. The decision, if left to the tennis professional, is to a large extent a matter of that pro's point of view. Most will be happy to discuss the issue with you.

Before your child can begin to use a specific grip, he must know how to hold the racket correctly. The demonstrations on the next three pages show two methods for teaching your child how to hold the racket.

SLIDING HAND GRIP METHOD

Step 1. Have your child place her throwing hand, with fingers extended, on the racket face.

Step 2. Ask her to slide her hand down the throat until her palm reaches the racket handle. The resulting grip should duplicate that shown in the demonstration above. Again, your child will change her hand position as necessary to suit her chosen grip.

SHAKING HANDS GRIP METHOD

Step 1. To set up the correct grip, ask your child to shake hands with you or with another child.

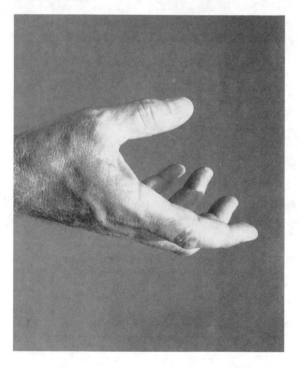

Step 2. Without changing finger and hand shape, your child should remove his hand from the handshake position. Remind your child of the imaginary V line on his hand.

Step 3. Place the racket in your child's hand. The fingers should spread loosely around the handle. To locate the V properly on the handle you must know which grip (eastern, continental, etc.) your child will use, since each grip has different requirements.

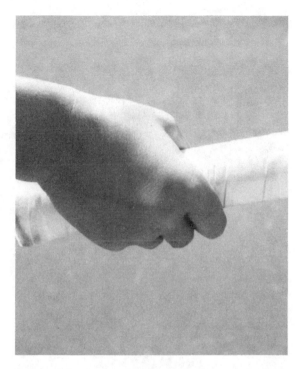

THE FOREHAND

If a right-handed player hits a ball that is on the right side of his body, the shot is called a forehand, and vice versa for a left-handed player.

The forehand stroke involves six basic steps, which are the same no matter how the racket is held. These steps, illustrated on pages 29-34, are:

1. Ready position
2. Racket back
3. Turn to the side
4. Step in
5. Hit
6. Follow through

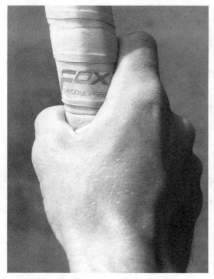

Eastern forehand grip.

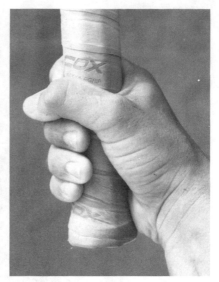

Western forehand grip.

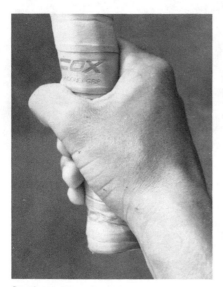

Semiwestern grip.

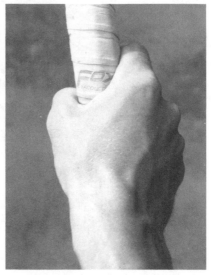

Continental grip.

Eastern or Continental Forehands

The eastern forehand grip is the single most commonly recommended grip for beginning players and is considered to be the "orthodox" approach. The continental grip, which is actually a compromise between the eastern forehand and the eastern backhand, became popular when used by Australian players, including Lew Hoad and Rod Laver.

The swing for both grips is essentially the same. The demonstration on page 29 shows how a forehand should be hit if a child is holding the racket with an eastern or a continental grip.

Western Forehands

A player holding the racket with either a semiwestern or full western grip hits the ball much differently than for the eastern or continental grips. Much more wrist movement is involved and the swing and the follow-through are different, as you can see in this demonstration. The palm of the hand is said to be "under" the racket with a western grip (see page 26), and the racket face and throat are no longer parallel to the ground, among other things. The basic steps, however, are the same: ready position, racket back, turn to the side, step in, hit and follow through.

FOREHAND PRACTICE POINTER

With the continental grip, the wrist should be kept in a nearly fixed position throughout the swing. If your child "snaps" or "rolls" his wrist either upward or downward, try to correct the swing and, if you have problems, discuss it with the pro. A player using an eastern grip has slightly more wrist movement, but there shouldn't be any wrist rolling or snapping. A good training technique is to ask the player to "catch" the racket in his non-racket hand as shown here.

GRIP TROUBLESHOOTING

Mistakes made with the forehand grip must be corrected immediately or your child's progress will be inhibited. The three most common problems are illustrated below.

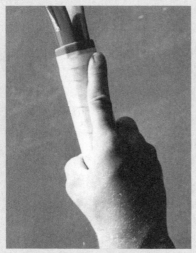

Since children's wrists are weak, they try to compensate by putting a forefinger behind the racket.

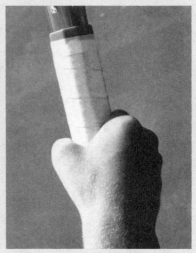

Notice how the fingers are all bunched together. This is called a *hammer* grip.

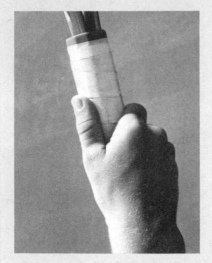

Some children find it more comfortable to put the thumb on top of the racket. This is also an incorrect grip.

HITTING THE FOREHAND (EASTERN OR CONTINENTAL GRIP)

Step 1. Ready Position. The correct stance is feet parallel to the net and a shoulder width apart, knees bent, weight forward, and racket at chest level.

Step 2. Racket Back. The non-racket hand releases the racket handle. The racket moves straight back, in a semicircular fashion. The racket must stay parallel to the ground and the racket face perpendicular to the ground. The racket head points straight at the back fence with the elbow bent slightly. The non-racket hand ends up pointing toward the oncoming ball.

Step 3. Turn to the Side and Step In. While the racket moves backward, your child pivots on the balls of her feet so her hips and shoulders are sideways to the net. A right-handed player then steps toward the net with the left foot, and vice versa for the left-handed player.

Step 4. Hit the Ball. As the racket moves forward to hit the ball, your child's weight shifts gradually onto the front foot. The swing begins slightly below where impact with the ball will occur (roughly around the front hip), and ends slightly above contact point. This swing hits "up" on the ball and creates the lift necessary to get the ball over the net. The semicircular swing should be evenly timed. The arm is fully extended and the racket throat is parallel to the ground at the moment of impact.

Step 5. Follow Through. The racket face remains perpendicular to the ground. The racket points at the opponent when the swing is complete. No steps are taken after the shot is hit, and your child should pause momentarily holding the finish position as in a pose before returning to the ready position, which requires moving the front foot back next to the back foot.

HITTING THE FOREHAND (WESTERN GRIP)

Step 1. Ready Position. Remember, feet parallel to the net and a shoulder width apart, knees bent, weight forward, and racket at chest level.

Step 2. Racket Back. Release the non-racket hand. Bring the racket straight back in a semicircular fashion, keeping the racket throat parallel to the ground. Point the racket at the back fence. Notice how the racket face is more "open," i.e., angled up slightly. The non-racket hand points at the oncoming ball.

Step 3. Turn to the Side and Step In. Turn sideways and step in with the foot opposite the side of the body the ball is on. While moving the racket forward to contact the ball, shift the weight gradually onto the front foot.

Step 4. Hit the Ball. Begin the swing slightly below the point of impact. Contact with the ball is made in front of the body. Notice that the hips rotate with the shoulders as the arm swings through and makes contact with the ball. Notice also that at the moment of impact the racket face is perpendicular to the ground, just as it is with the eastern and continental forehands.

Step 5. Follow Through. After contact, the wrist "rolls" over and the racket face is closed, i.e., slightly facing the ground.

Step 6. Follow Through. The racket head ends up just in front of the child's shoulder. With a particularly hard swing, the racket head could even end up behind the shoulder. Some pros teach children to finish all shots with their elbows up in front of their faces.

FOREHAND TROUBLESHOOTING

These photos show three of the most common mistakes that are made by children when learning how to hit the forehand.

This open stance results in a weak swing and very limited ability to reach and hit balls away from the body. Your child must step toward the net on the foot opposite the side of the body the ball is on.

After the swing the racket should be pointed at the net, not wrapped around the body.

Choking up on the racket occurs when the hand is too far up on the handle.

THE BACKHAND

If a right-handed player hits a ball that is on the left side of his body, the shot is called a backhand, and the reverse is true for a left-handed player. A child needs strong wrists to play tennis, and it takes more strength in the wrists to hit a backhand than a forehand. For that reason, most players have a stronger forehand than backhand. Since few children younger than ten have the necessary strength in their wrists to control the racket and hit the backhand with one hand, many pros have young beginners use both hands to hit the backhand. Some children, such as a few of Jimmy Evert's children, most notably Chris, who is clearly one of the greatest women players to have ever played the game, have done quite well using two hands as adult players.

With a two-handed swing, a child moves the racket arm in the same way as a one-handed backhand should be hit, as far as the elbow and wrist movement is concerned. If desired, your child can change from a two-handed swing to a one-handed swing when his wrists become strong enough to handle the backhand with one hand. Whether to begin as a two-handed player or to hit the backhand with one hand, which is the orthodox approach, is something you can discuss with the pro.

Figure Eight Swing

The figure eight swing was considered the classical way to hit a forehand or a backhand. It acquired its name because the swing resembles a sideways eight. As play on faster court surfaces becomes more prevalent, players simplify the swing so it is a straight back and straight forward swing, because the ball is traveling faster and there is less time to swing. The classic figure eight swing is seen most on slow surfaces, such as clay.

One-Handed Backhand

The one-handed backhand, illustrated on pages 39-41, means simply that the player hits a backhand with only one hand on the racket handle at the time of contact. Since one-handed and two-handed backhands are hit differently, they will be discussed separately.

As described on page 38, depending on which grip is used, your child may have to change the position of his hand on the racket to hit a backhand. To do this, your child uses the opposite hand to hold the racket while releasing pressure of the dominant hand. He then adjusts the V to the desired position on the racket handle. Players who hold the racket with a *continental* grip won't need to change grips on any shots. The full western grip, below left, also is the same for all shots, although this grip is rarely seen anymore, especially on the backhand, and is not recommended. As hard as it may be to imagine, with this grip the ball is hit on the same side of the racket face for both the forehand and backhand.

Players who hold the racket with an *eastern* forehand grip shift their backhand grips so the V on their racket hand meets the left edge of the racket handle as shown below right.

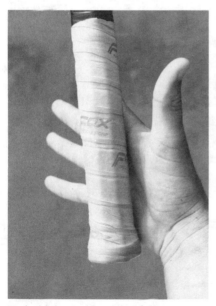 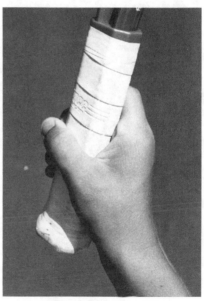

To hold the racket with a full western grip, the hand should be outstretched and parallel to the ground. Lay the racket, with the face perpendicular to the ground, on top of the palm, as shown.

For an eastern backhand grip, the V formed by the thumb and index finger is shifted left of the handle's center bevel, to the middle of the next bevel.

Two-Handed Backhand

The two-handed backhand grip means simply that the player hits the ball with two hands on the racket handle at the time of contact. It is similar to the way a baseball player grips a bat with both hands touching and without fingers interlocking or overlapping. Contact with the ball occurs at a slightly different location than with a one-handed backhand, and there is much more body—especially hip—movement.

Summary of Grip Comparisons

Eastern: This is the most orthodox grip. It involves a change of hand position on the racket from the forehand to the backhand. It is good for ground strokes, and, on an advanced level, for net play and serve and volley.

Continental: This needs no change of grip for any shots. On an advanced level it is good for serve and volley game and for hitting low balls, as on fast courts. It is difficult to create much spin since the wrist is in a nearly fixed position, and it is harder to hit balls above the waist with much power.

Semiwestern: For this grip, a hand change from the forehand grip is necessary to hit a backhand. On an advanced level it is excellent for generating spin and power but not for volleys or serves. While it is more difficult to use on fast courts, this grip is becoming increasingly popular.

Full western: This grip involves extremely exaggerated wrist movement and very heavy topspin shots. Players who used this grip in the past would hit the backhand with the same grip and with the same side of the racket face. It is very poor for serves, volleys and overheads and is much less commonly seen than any of the three grips listed above.

ONE-HANDED EASTERN BACKHAND

Step 1. Ready Position. Children who hit the backhand with one hand may have a slightly different ready position from players with a two-handed backhand. They do not have to, but they might prefer to place their non-racket hand in the area of the throat to help them balance the racket, shown left. This is the conventional approach. However, they may place the non-racket hand next to the racket hand, just as a two-handed player does, shown below.

Step 2. Racket Back and Turn to the Side. Regardless of where the non-racket hand is placed for a backhand, both hands remain on the racket until the racket is brought back. The steps are the same (racket back and turn to the side).

Step 3. Step In. The one-handed player lets go of the racket with the non-racket hand as she begins to move the racket forward to make contact with the ball.

Step 4. Hit the Ball. At the moment of impact the arm is fully extended. Notice that the wrist must be strong so the racket will not turn or give way upon contact.

Step 5. Follow Through. The follow-through is the same as with the forehand, except that the non-racket hand is pointing at the back fence. The result can be a spread-eagle effect, which is really quite picturesque.

WESTERN BACKHAND

Step 1. Assume the ready position.

Step 2. Draw the racket back and turn sideways to the net.

Step 3. Step in and prepare to hit the ball. Notice the high, racket back position.

Step 4. At impact, the racket face is perpendicular to the ground. Notice that the point of impact is farther in front of the body than with the eastern or continental backhand.

Step 5. Follow Through. Notice the extended position of the arm and how the right shoulder opens up to the net.

TWO-HANDED BACKHAND

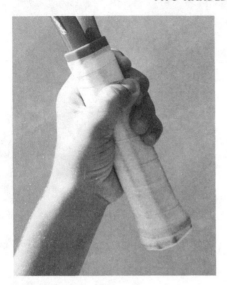

Step 1. To teach the child who holds the racket with an eastern grip how to grip the racket with two hands, ask the child to put her left hand on the racket just as a left-handed player using an eastern forehand grip would do.

Step 2. Next, have the child put her racket hand on the racket just as she does to hit the forehand. As shown, the hands make contact, but the fingers do not interlock. A player who uses a continental grip grips the racket with the non-racket hand using a continental grip.

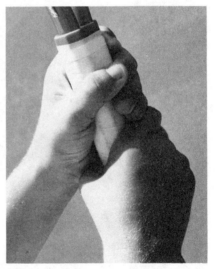

Step 3. Ready Position. The five sequential steps for hitting the backhand with two hands are the same as with a one-handed backhand.

Step 4. Racket Back and Turn to the Side.

Step 5. Step In.

Step 6. Hit the Ball. The spot where contact is made varies by a few inches, but remains in the vicinity of the hips.

Step 7. Follow Through.

BACKHAND TROUBLESHOOTING

Here is the most common mistake you are likely to see a beginning child commit on the backhand stroke.

Sarah is hitting the ball way too far in front of her and probably has her thumb up behind the racket. Also, her elbow is too far in front of her body, which could produce an injury such as tennis elbow.

THE SERVE

The serve is the shot that a player hits to begin a point. It is the only stroke in tennis that a player can completely control. Every other stroke is determined by what type of shot an opponent hits and where. The serve is also the only stroke in tennis that can be practiced without an opponent, backboard, ball machine or other aid.

It is important to develop the mechanics of the serve very slowly. Don't rush your child into learning how to serve and play games too soon. Your pro will undoubtedly spend weeks on the service toss alone before asking the children to actually try to hit the ball. If the toss is not in the right location, your child will swing the racket incorrectly and develop a habit that will become harder and harder to break.

The racket should be held with either the continental grip or the eastern backhand grip. However, some younger children simply cannot control the racket with either grip and must use a grip similar to a western forehand grip to hit the ball. This is acceptable as long as you and your child understand that he should change his grip when he gets stronger.

SERVE PRACTICE POINTERS

- Before your child tosses the ball, have him reach up as high as he can with his racket arm while holding the racket. Explain that the ball should be tossed about two feet above his outstretched arm and racket. This shows how high the toss needs to be.
- Before your child hits the ball, have him watch where the tossed ball lands. The ball should land about twelve inches ahead of his front foot and about twelve inches to the side (to the right side for right-handed players and to the left for left-handers).
- Explain the serve as a four-step motion:

  Step 1: Drop the hands.

  Step 2: Bring the racket arm to back-scratch position and extend tossing arm.

  Step 3: Hit the ball.

  Step 4: Follow through.

Step 1. The Stance. Position the front foot at a forty-five-degree angle to the base line and just inches behind the line. A right-handed player puts his left foot forward and vice versa for a left-hander. The back foot angles in the same direction as the front foot, but about a foot or two behind the base line. The feet are a shoulder width apart and the weight is on the front foot. Point the racket toward the opponent with the racket head in the mid-section area. While holding only one ball, the non-racket hand is in the vicinity of the throat of the racket.

Step 2. Holding the Ball. The ball is held loosely in the fingers of the non-racket hand.

Step 3. The Swing. When beginning the swing, your child moves both hands downward at the same time. The tossing hand makes contact with the thigh area of the front leg at approximately the same time that the racket arm reaches the down position. The racket points toward the ground and slightly to the rear.

Step 4. Next, both hands move upward at the same time. The racket hand moves up until it is in the back-scratch position shown here. This happens at approximately the same time as the tossing arm becomes fully extended. The arm motion is smooth and continuous.

Step 5. When the tossing arm is fully extended, the child releases or tosses the ball. After the tossed ball reaches its peak and begins to descend, the racket hand moves forward from the back-scratch position to make contact with the tossed ball. At the time of contact the racket arm is fully extended.

Step 6. The child finishes the swing with her racket pointing slightly to the rear and on the opposite side of the body.

Step 7. Follow through by stepping into the court with the back foot and adjusting the grip, if necessary, to prepare for either a forehand or backhand.

SERVE TROUBLESHOOTING

John is standing with his body facing the net. His feet are in an incorrect position, causing his whole body to be in the wrong position. The correct position for the feet is shown right.

John is making contact with the ball at nose level. Contact should be made when his arm is fully extended above his head.

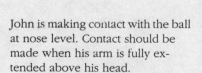

THE VOLLEY

When a player hits a ball before it bounces, the shot is referred to as a *volley*. Most volleys are hit inside the service line, close to the net. The most important thing to keep in mind when practicing the volley with your child is that it is not a swing, like the forehand or backhand. It is more like a "punch," that is, a short, jabbing motion. The forehand volley should be hit as follows:

Your child should hold the racket with a continental grip, if possible, since there is not as much time to change grips at the net as there is if your child is standing at the base line. It is best to learn the correct volleying grip right from the start, but this may be difficult. At first, since he won't be challenged by fast action, let your child hold the racket for the volley as he does for the forehand and backhand, provided he is using the eastern grip. Players using western grips should be encouraged to use the continental grip, even though it will be difficult, because few advanced players have been able to effectively volley with a western grip. However, there are certainly many players who use the western grip and enjoy the social and recreational aspects of the game. I suggest you discuss this situation with your pro if a problem develops.

THE BACKHAND VOLLEY

The backhand volley, which involves the same steps and technique as the forehand volley, moves the elbow across the body to get in the contact position. The backhand volley requires more strength in the wrist to hit the ball, so it is more difficult for children.

THE HALF VOLLEY

When a ball hits at or near your child's feet and he is not able to hit the ball before it bounces, the return shot is called a *half volley*. It is a ball hit on a short hop. The most important thing to keep in mind is that your child must bend his knees and get as low to the ground as possible to hit a half volley. The grip for the half volley is the same as for the volley.

THE VOLLEY

Step 1. The Stance and Swing. Position your child about a yard inside the service line. The ready position is the same as with the forehand and the backhand, except the racket head is held slightly higher, closer to the shoulder area. The most important thing to emphasize about the swing is that the racket is not brought back any farther than the shoulders, which are parallel to the net. The racket head is at shoulder level. The shoulders do not turn as the child brings the racket back. As the ball approaches, your child steps in with the opposite foot. In other words, if the ball is on the left side of his body, he steps in with the right foot. If the ball is on the right side of his body, he steps in with the left foot, just as with the forehand or backhand. He will necessarily rotate his hips to the side in the process.

A side view shows clearly where the racket should be positioned at the moment of impact.

Step 2. Step In. As the ball approaches, the racket moves forward to make contact. At the moment of impact, the arm is extended, the elbow slightly bent and the weight is on the front foot.

A side view shows the racket's position when the volley is finished.

Step 3. Follow Through. The follow-through should be extremely short. The entire swing on the volley should cover less than two feet in a forward direction.

BACKHAND VOLLEY

Step 1. Ready Position. Remember that the racket head is held slightly higher and closer to the shoulders than for the forehand and the backhand.

Step 2. Racket Back. The racket moves back only as far as the shoulders.

Step 3. Step In and Hit. As the ball approaches, your child steps toward it with the foot farthest from the ball.

HALF VOLLEY

Step 1. The Stance. The ready position for the half volley is the same as for the volley: Stand a yard inside the service line with the racket at chest level.

A side view shows the position of the racket awaiting the oncoming ball.

Step 2. The Swing. Step forward with the foot opposite the side of the body that the ball is on, and bend that knee to get down as low to the ground as possible. The racket is taken back even less than for a regular volley. The wrist is firm, with the racket held in a stationary position awaiting the oncoming ball.

Step 3. Push the Ball. At the moment of impact, the racket face must be angled up so the ball will clear the net. The racket is pushed forward. How much push is given will determine how far the ball travels.

A side view shows the angled racket position upon follow-through.

VOLLEY PRACTICE POINTERS

- The player needs to change the angle of the racket face in relation to the ground, depending on where contact with the ball is made. The face of the racket is perpendicular to the ground if contact with the ball is made between the waist and shoulders. If contact is made below the net, the face of the racket is angled up so the ball will go over the net. For a ball higher than the shoulders, the angle is slightly downward.

- When you coach a number of beginning children, position them within a foot of the net. Tell them to turn to the side, step in, and position their rackets as shown below. Next, toss the balls from close range. This makes it easier for children to learn that the volley is hit with a short, jabbing motion, rather than a full swing.

VOLLEY TROUBLESHOOTING

The best grip for the volley is the continental, which uses the same grip for forehand and backhand volleys. The eastern grip is acceptable, but it requires different grips for forehand and backhand. If your child uses a semi-western or full western grip to hit a forehand, he should be encouraged to use either the continental or the eastern grip right from the start for a volley. Here are common volleying mistakes.

Here again, the player should step in with the left foot. His shoulders should be perpendicular to the net.

The racket and the arm should be angled slightly, as shown on page 56, rather than in straight alignment. Also, the player should step in with his left foot and be sideways to the net for this forehand volley.

The back of the player's wrist should face the net, with the opposite racket face—the correct side—toward ball.

HALF VOLLEY TROUBLESHOOTING

Stiff knees and a too-erect body are common problems associated with the half volley. Remind your child to relax, bend his knees, and get as low to the ground as possible.

THE OVERHEAD

When a player must reach high above his head to hit a ball, the stroke is called an *overhead*. The overhead shot should be hit with a motion similar to the service motion. Normally, it is hit when a child is close to the net, after an opponent attempts to loft the ball over the net player's head. The grip for the overhead is the same as for the serve.

OVERHEAD PRACTICE POINTERS

- The most common mistake made by children while learning to hit an overhead is letting the ball drop too low before making contact with the ball. Your child's arm should be fully extended at the moment of impact. Contact with the ball should occur at about six inches to a foot or so in front of the shoulder of the hitting arm.
- Children hit the overhead virtually the same way they hit the serve. If your child is not getting his arm fully extended on the overhead or the serve, practice the baseball pitching game referred to in chapter five, but begin by having your child extend his arms fully above his head before throwing the ball. This can be practiced anywhere, and is really nothing more than playing catch. You can use a tennis ball, baseball or football, since the throwing motions are very similar.
- The second most common mistake made by children who are just learning how to hit the overhead is incorrectly shifting their weight onto the back foot after hitting the ball. The weight should be shifted onto the front foot. Although not necessary, a player may even let the back foot step forward after contact is made, which ensures a forward weight shift.
- The third most common mistake is failing to turn to the side when preparing to hit the overhead, which results in hitting the ball with both feet facing the net, in a side-by-side fashion. A player should point the non-racket hand at the ball, just as soon as the player recognizes that a lob has been hit, which simulates the toss for the serve, turn to the side and get the racket in the back-scratch position.

THE OVERHEAD

Step 1. The Stance. Position your child approximately one yard inside the service line.

Step 2. Preparation. To prepare to hit a lob, or a lofted ball, your child places his racket in the same back-scratch position as used for the serve, moving his feet as quickly as possible to get under the ball or slightly in front of the spot where the ball would otherwise land. The non-racket hand points at the ball while it is in the air, helping your child properly align his body to the arc of the oncoming ball. The shoulders and hips turn sideways to the net, and the feet angle as they do for the serve. The weight is on the back foot until he is ready to swing.

Step 3. The Swing. The swing is timed so that the arm is fully extended when the ball is hit, just as with the serve. The weight is shifted onto the front foot as the child swings to make contact with the ball.

Step 4. Follow Through. The swing finishes with the racket on the opposite side of the body, as with the serve. However, the child does not follow through by stepping forward with the back foot as is done with the serve. The child returns to the ready position by moving the front foot backward.

Chapter Five

HOW TO CONDUCT A PRACTICE SESSION

Before leaving your house to practice, try to make certain that a court is available. Reserve a court, if possible. Nothing dampens energy and enthusiasm more than waiting an hour or more before getting on a court.

In deciding how long to practice, find a happy medium to best meet the mutual wants and needs of you and your child. Most important, since you won't be happy if you know you should be or would rather be doing something else, schedule the sessions at a time of day that suits you. It is best if you can set aside a certain hour on any given day, and make it a regular activity that you and your child look forward to. The practice sessions and lessons should be things your child wants to do rather than being required to do them.

Not all days are sunny and warm. On those days when your child is tired or grumpy or otherwise distracted, make the best of the situation and, if necessary, end the sessions early. There will be days when some discipline is required, and on those occasions you must exercise self-restraint and not ruin the supportive atmosphere you are trying to create. This will be difficult at times. Reward good behavior with Popsicles or soft drinks. Treats also help end the session on a happy note. Your child's smile, after being rewarded with a Popsicle or other treat, can make your day. Now that you are fully briefed and organized, you are ready to take to the court.

ORGANIZING THE SESSIONS
Before walking onto the court, you should have a good idea of what you want to practice and how you intend to accomplish your goal. As you progress, you can vary your sessions as you see fit to

meet the needs and desires of your child. For beginning youngsters I suggest the following program, which can be completed in half an hour.

- Lead warmup exercises, such as jumping jacks and toe touching, for a few minutes.
- Have your child run lines (see page 91).
- Have your child bounce balls and squeeze balls for a minute or two (see pages 86-87).
- Practice the forehand and backhand strokes. Toss balls to your child so he can swing his racket and hit the balls with as little movement as possible, other than to step in. Start with five balls. Repeat as desired. For the first few weeks, spend most of your time on this drill.
- Take a water break.
- Have your child perform a running exercise, such as a line identification drill (see page 85).
- If you are working with more than one child, play a competitive game such as most forehands or backhands over the net or the elimination game. If it is just you and your child, count the number of balls over and try to set a "record" each time (see page 82).
- Conduct a competitive running game or, if it is only you and your child, time the exercise.
- Adjourn and give out a reward.

As your child improves, I suggest you gradually add the following exercises to your program and increase court time accordingly.

- Practice the volley.
- Practice the serve, which may mean simply practicing the toss or throwing the ball.
- Practice the overhead, which may simply mean having your child catch the ball.
- Play different competitive or fun games (see pages 82-85).

HITTING DRILLS

On the following pages are six court diagrams that show where you and four children should stand for hitting drills. If you and your child are practicing alone, your child should stand in the center of the area where the series of four Xs appears.

Begin by positioning yourself at the net on the same side of the court as your child, who should stand on the service line, as shown in Drill One.

Toss balls from this position for your child to hit as forehands and backhands. Once he is able to hit the ball reasonably well from that position, change both your positions and progress through Drills Two through Six until you are on your base line and he is on the opposite base line. Beginning in Drill Four you should use your racket to hit, not toss, balls to your child.

You will quickly discover that the farther away from your child you stand, the more variables come into play, such as speed of the ball, height of the bounce, location of the ball in relation to the body, and the timing of the swing. Change the pattern slowly and go back and forth from point to point. Challenge your child's abilities by moving farther away, then restore his confidence by returning to positions closer to him. You can expect an older child to advance through the positions much more quickly than a younger one, and for that reason, among others, it is best to have a group of children of approximately the same age if your child is in a practice group.

Hitting Drill One.

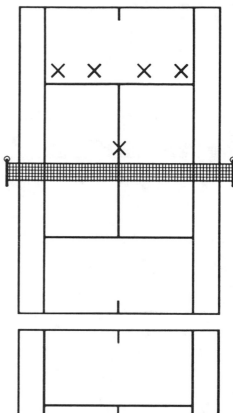

Hitting Drill Two.

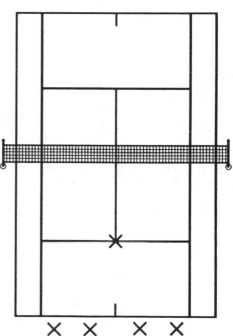

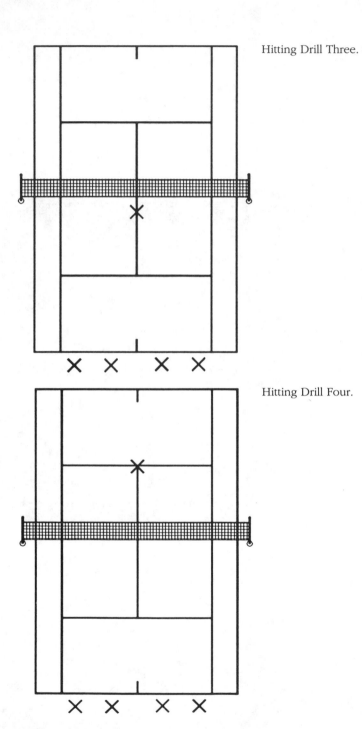

Hitting Drill Three.

Hitting Drill Four.

Hitting Drill Five.

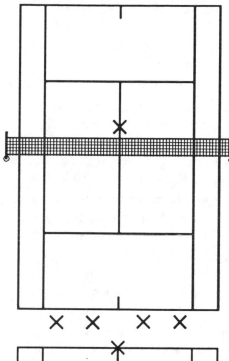

Hitting Drill Six.

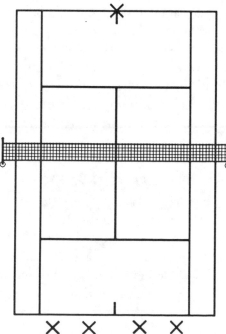

HOW TO THROW THE BALL

In the beginning, your goal is to make it as easy as possible for your child to hit the ball. You should consistently toss balls underhanded at the same speed and in the same location. Try to place the ball exactly where your child's racket should meet the ball.

The ball should bounce once before reaching a point approximately one yard to either side of the child, in the area of the mid-section. In the beginning, don't throw overhand and don't use your racket. The accuracy of your toss will more than likely determine whether your child hits the ball. This is not as easy as it sounds. It will take practice and concentration on your part.

As you change your position on the court or change the way you throw (and eventually hit) the ball, your child will have to move his feet to adjust to the changing location of the ball. It won't be as easy for you to make the ball bounce to the perfect spot. This process is similar to the way a child learns to judge a fly ball in baseball. It takes time. If you ever feel that there is no hope your child will develop into a tennis player, go watch a peewee baseball or teeball game. I am certain that it will improve your spirits.

As your child progresses, continue to try to make it as easy as possible for him to hit the ball. This will become even more difficult for you when you begin hitting a ball with your racket, which should occur when you move to the opposite side of the net in Drills Four through Six. Gradually, and sometimes imperceptibly, your child will improve. He will also become better at judging fly balls.

THROWING PRACTICE POINTER

Keep the ball hopper close to your non-tossing hand so you can easily replenish your supply of balls. The tossing motion is much like pitching a horseshoe or a softball. Stand with your feet apart and the foot opposite your tossing arm a step forward. The tossing arm extends fully behind you and points to the back court. As the arm swings forward it remains extended and your weight shifts forward.

HOW TO THROW THE BALL

Step 1. Hold the ball loosely and swing your arm back a comfortable distance.

Step 2. With a smooth motion, swing your arm forward in a straight line.

Step 3. Continue the relaxed forward motion, finishing the toss with your arm at head height.

ADDING MOVEMENT TO THE DRILLS

Once your child learns how to hold the racket and swing it correctly, you need to add movement to the hitting exercises. Here are some good movement drills:

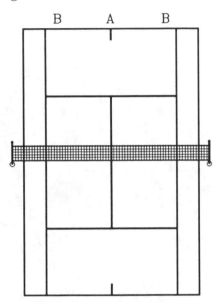

Two-Position Drill. Position your child in the center of the court on the base line (position A). Throw or hit a ball so your child hits a forehand shot from the middle of the base line. After your child hits the shot, he sidesteps quickly to either of the two corners of the court (position B). When he reaches the corner and stops, throw a ball to that corner so he can hit a second shot from this new position.

Three-Position Drill. Position your child in one corner of the court, on the base line, and have him hit either a forehand or backhand (position A). After hitting the shot, the child sidesteps to the center of the court and hits a second shot (position B). After hitting the second shot, he sidesteps to the opposite corner to hit a third shot (position C).

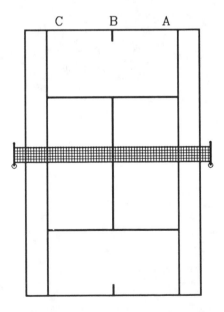

Four-Position Drill. Position your child in the center of the court on the base line (position A). Have the child hit either a forehand or a backhand from that position. The child then sidesteps to either corner for a second shot (position B). He sidesteps back to the center for the third shot (position C). He sidesteps to the opposite corner for a fourth and final shot (position D).

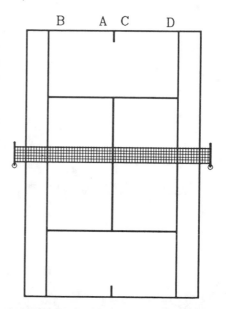

Shadow Drills. An additional child or children can be included in the above exercises, and in most other drills, by simply asking the next child or children in line to "shadow" the child doing the drill. A shadow lines up five feet behind the child performing the drill and imitates every movement. This helps to keep all of the children active in the session.

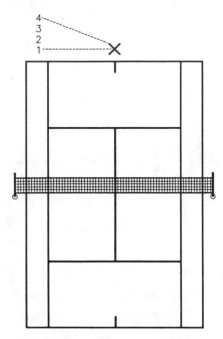

Circle Hit. If you have three or four children to work with, line them up in single file behind either alley. The first child sidesteps to the middle of the court, hits a shot, and runs to the end of the line. As the first child is running to the end of the line, the second child sidesteps to the center of the court, hits a ball, and then runs to the end of line; and so forth. Fast action and constant movement make this exercise fun.

Combination Drill. One child hits a serve (position A); then, regardless of where the serve is hit, toss balls so that he hits a forehand from position B and then a backhand from the opposite corner (position C) of the base line. He then runs to (or "rushes") the net and hits a forehand volley (position D), a backhand volley (position E), and an overhead (position F).

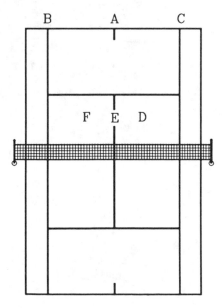

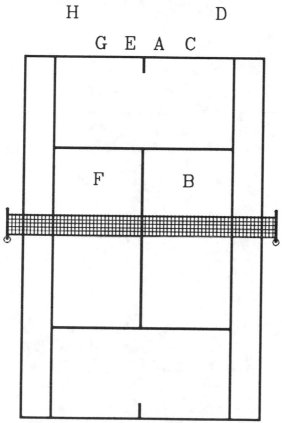

Up-and-Back Drills. A child stands in the center of the court on the base line and hits a backhand from the center of the court (position A). He moves forward to the service line and hits another backhand shot (position B). He then back-steps to the center of the base line and hits another backhand (position C). He then back-steps three steps to hit a ball that lands on the base line and bounces deep with another backhand (position D). He returns to center position to hit a forehand (position E). He runs up to hit a shallow forehand near the service line (position F). He back-steps to the base line to hit another forehand (position G). He then back-steps three steps behind the base line to hit a final forehand (position H). Note: This drill can be broken up into a number of smaller types of drills involving fewer shots.

SIDE-TO-SIDE DRILL

Step 1. Position a child in the center of the court on the base line.

Step 2. Have the child sidestep a few steps, toward the appropriate corner, to hit a forehand.

Step 3. She then side-steps toward the opposite corner to hit a backhand.

Step 4. Repeat, without stopping, as many times as desired.

WINDSHIELD WIPERS

Step 1. Position two children behind the base line, one child halfway between the center mark and singles line on one side, and the other child halfway between the center mark and singles line on the other side of the court. The children will mirror each other.

Step 2. Throw a ball to either child to hit; the other child swings just as if he were hitting a ball thrown to him.

Step 3. Next, throw a ball to the other child to hit on the opposite side of the body. The effect will be like that of windshield wipers on a car.

CROSSOVER FEED-IN

Step 1. Position four children behind the base line as shown.

Step 2. Have one player sidestep to the middle and hit either a forehand or a backhand.

Step 3. She then sidesteps to the end of the line on the other side of the court.

Step 4. The first player in line on the other side of the court then sidesteps to the middle to hit a shot and goes to the end of the other line and so forth.

GAMES TO PLAY FOR COMPETITION OR FUN

Competitive Games

Although some parents want to downplay the importance of competition at this early stage, I believe you will find it useful to inject some competition into the practice sessions to maintain interest and justify the rewards you give out after the sessions. You can make all games more fun by heaping praise and encouragement on each child, even though only one ends up winning. These games are most helpful when you are coaching a group of children. However, you can use some of the games with your child alone by keeping an ongoing record of his scores and rewarding his progress as the scores improve. Some competitive games are listed below.

Most balls hit over the net. Toss five balls to each child on the forehand side first and then the backhand. Tally the number of balls each hits over the net. Later, you can add volleys and the overhead.

Most balls bounced off the racket. The children hold their rackets correctly and bounce balls either up in the air or down off the ground to see who can bounce the most balls in a row.

Most balls dropped and hit over the net. The children drop balls from waist level to see who can hit the most balls over the net.

Most serves hit into the correct service box. Each child hits five serves.

Mini-tennis. The children play tennis by standing on the service lines rather than the base lines, using the same rules, scoring and movement as if the entire court were being used.

Elimination games. Position the children at the service line. (As they progress in skill level, they can stand at the base line.) Toss a ball to each child to hit as a forehand or backhand. Any child who doesn't put the ball over the net is eliminated until one child is left as the winner of the game.

Since your purpose is to make the time spent on the court as much fun as possible for everyone, don't discourage those who are not doing as well as others. Sometimes rewards should be given for best attitude, most effort, or most balls picked up. Best of all, reward *each* child for something done well.

Fun Games

Fun games are primarily intended to be pure and simple fun, but they also serve a secondary purpose of either exercise or stroke technique development. The number and variety of games you can play is limited only by your imagination. The single most important ingredient to making a game fun is the attitude with which you begin the activity and with which the children pursue the activity. The games described here involve several children, but most are appropriate for you and your child to play also. Some examples of fun games are:

Baseball (Hitting): For this game, the children attempt to hit a tennis ball over the net and into the opposite court. The children's skill level determines whether they stand on either the service line or on the base line and whether you toss or hit the balls to them. The children can hit forehands or backhands. A ball hit in either service box is a single (base hit). A ball hit over the service line but more than one yard from the base line is a double. A ball landing in either of the two alleys is a triple. A ball landing within one yard of the base line is a home run. Any ball that doesn't clear the net or lands outside the court is a foul ball. You can set up some tennis ball cans or other objects to define the home run area. If you have four children, the children could run the bases to make it even more fun, or you could play two children against the other two.

Baseball (Pitching): Begin with the children standing single file in the center of the base line. Position yourself on the other side of the net in either service box. The younger children can stand on the service line, if necessary. After a short warm-up to loosen their arms, play a game of balls and strikes. If a child can throw the ball in the service box, it is a strike. Anything out of the service box or any ball that does not go over the net is a ball. As they throw the ball, remind them that the throwing motion is much like the service motion. It is most important that the arm be fully extended at the time the ball is released.

Baseball (Catching): Position the children along the service line while you stand on the opposite side of the net on the other service line. Hit a ball to each of the children, one at a time, for them to catch. A ball should be hit like a short lob, just high enough so the child can reach up and catch it, but not so deep as to go over his head. A ball that is caught is an out. Any ball that is not caught is a hit. You can have all the children play as a team against you or the children can play against each other. Try to have the children catch the ball with their hands over their heads, as this will better prepare them for hitting overheads. For the little children, catching the ball on one bounce is a challenge. It also helps them learn to judge the bounce or figure out how it will bounce and where.

Baseball (Pitching and Catching): Have the children throw the ball to you, as described on page 83 in Baseball (Pitching). When a child throws a strike, hit the ball back over the net so that it bounces once before reaching the child who tries to catch it.

Running Races: If you have two or more children to work with, you can play a number of different running games.

- Distance—The children race along the perimeter of the court(s), assuming this will not disturb neighboring players. If necessary, they can run on the outside of the fence, or in any playgrounds or fields nearby. If they are running on the court, start the children on opposite sides of the net to avoid a possible collision.
- Speed—The children race from one side of the court to the other, or from the net to the back fence.
- Running lines—The children stand on opposite sides of the net on the base line. Starting at the same time, they race against each other while running the lines of the court, using the technique described on page 88.
- Relay races—If you have four children, two race against the other two by running relay races around the court. Use a ball or a tennis racket as a baton. Start the teams on opposite sides of the net.
- Balancing a ball on the racket—The children stand at the back fence, rackets in hand. First, each balances a ball on his racket. Next, they walk or run as fast as they can to the net and back

without losing control of the ball. The first one back to the fence wins.

Basketball (Horse): As in basketball, the game begins when one player chooses a shot to hit, from any location on his side of the court, and attempts to do so. You can toss or hit the ball to the child or they can drop and hit it. If the child is able to hit the ball over the net into the opposite court, the other children must make the same shot or else they are given a letter. Once a child spells "horse," he is out of the game. The child left in the game, after all the others have spelled "horse," is the winner. You can make up any name for your game, and you can use a name with any number of letters in it, such as "ace" or "champ" or "winner." Make the game more difficult by requiring the children to call their shot or to say where the ball will land.

Basketball (Lay-up Drill): In the event you have access to a basketball hoop, you can practice lay-ups, as in basketball, while practicing the toss for the serve. The children stand within a foot or two of the basket and attempt to toss the ball into the basket, using their non-racket hand, in an underhand motion. Tell them not to release the ball until their arms are fully extended, which is the proper motion for the toss in tennis as well as the lay-up in basketball.

Basketball (Dribbling): The children bounce the ball onto the ground using their rackets, just as they would bounce a basketball. After they get good enough, they can have races while bouncing the ball.

Name That Line: The children line up at the fence at the back of the court, facing the net. They run forward or sideways to whatever part of the court you call out. If the line called is behind them, they will need to back-step to get to it. (Back-stepping is running backward while keeping the head and body facing the net. The children need to be careful so as not to fall backward.) If the line called is to the side, they should sidestep to it while staying on a line. Call out the service line, net, base line, alley, singles line, doubles line, etc., and alternate so that children will be able to easily identify the names of the lines on the court.

Chapter Six

WHAT CHILDREN CAN PRACTICE ON THEIR OWN

There is no substitute for practice, period. No matter how many lessons your child takes or how many hours you spend on a court with him, he needs to practice countless hours with friends or alone. If your child enjoys playing tennis, the hours of practice will be hours of fun. The following are some good ways to practice.

DRILLS TO STRENGTHEN THE WRIST AND FOREARM

The most important muscles for a child to develop while learning to play tennis are in the wrist and forearm. The two best exercises for your child to perform at every session, and as often as possible at home, are squeezing balls and bouncing a ball with the racket. The latter also helps to develop eye-hand coordination.

Bouncing Balls

Using the correct grip, bounce (on the ground) a ball off the racket face. After bouncing the ball ten times in succession, increase the target to twenty-five and then to fifty.

Another drill is to bounce the ball into the air about two feet. Again, after this is done ten times, increase the target to twenty-five and then to fifty.

Once your child can do the first two exercises, he should bounce the ball off the opposite side of the racket face. This should be done both in the air and off the ground.

Next, alternate the bounce off one side of the racket face and then the other.

Squeezing Balls

Your child puts one ball in each hand and squeezes for a count of five and then releases pressure. Repeat the exercise ten times. This exercise should be done daily.

JUMPING ROPE

This is a great exercise for timing, quickness and endurance, in addition to being fun. Begin to teach your child to jump rope by having him hold two ropes, one in each hand. Have him swing the ropes in a circular fashion, in unison, while keeping his wrists near his waist. When he gets the motion and the timing of the swing, he discards one of the ropes and holds the two ends of the rope, one in each hand. Have him begin with five jumps, then ten, etc., performing one jump for one rotation.

RUNNING DRILLS

To play tennis, a child must run well and must possess speed, endurance and efficiency of motion. Your child can run on his own at any time and should be encouraged to do so to improve his speed and endurance. The running drills on page 88 are particularly suited to the movements needed on a tennis court.

Sprints

The child runs from the base line to the net and back-steps to the beginning point, stopping and resting briefly between repetitions.

USING A BALL MACHINE

Many tennis professionals have a ball machine for players to use for practice. A ball machine feeds balls to a player at whatever speed and in whatever location is desired. Usually the ball machine is placed on a secluded court so the balls don't go on other courts and bother other players. Using a ball machine gives you a chance to stand close to your child and help him practice correctly.

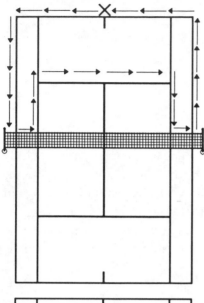

Running Lines. Starting on the base line at the center mark, your child sidesteps to the right, to the doubles line, at approximately ¾ speed. He then follows a circuit around the court: 1) runs forward to the net; 2) sidesteps to the singles line; 3) back-steps to the service line; 4) sidesteps across the service line to the opposite singles line; 5) runs to the net; 6) sidesteps to the doubles line; 7) back-steps to the base line; 8) sidesteps to the beginning position. Repeat this circuit two or three times.

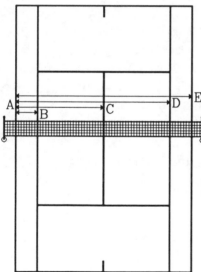

Shuttle Run. Your child starts on either of the doubles lines, no farther back from the net than the service line (position A). He then sidesteps to touch the nearest singles line (position B), and then back to the beginning; sidesteps to the center line (position C), and then back to the beginning; sidesteps to the opposite singles line (position D), and back to the beginning; sidesteps to the opposite doubles line (position E), and back to starting position.

FOREHAND DRILL

There are several ways your child can practice his forehand (or backhand—see page 90) alone. Interestingly, the way a child swings the racket when practicing is usually the way he will swing it when a ball is tossed or hit to him. Practice helps improve stroke technique as well as performance.

Step 1. Your child stands sideways to the net with his front foot almost touching the base line. He positions the racket in the racket-back position. Holding one ball in his non-racket hand, he extends this hand along the base line toward the spot where the racket should meet the ball.

Step 2. Since a child's arm is not long enough to reach the spot where contact should be made, he must toss the ball, allowing it to bounce one time, to the spot where the ball will be hit. He may need to step in with the front foot to make contact and hit the ball.

Step 3. He then follows through correctly and finishes with the racket pointing at his opponent, if he is using an eastern or continental grip. (See chapter four.)

BACKHAND DRILL

Step 1. Your child stands sideways to the net with the front foot touching the base line. Racket is in the racket-back position. Holding one ball in the non-racket hand, she extends her tossing arm (place tossing arm over and above the racket arm) along the base line toward the spot where the racket should meet the ball. As with the forehand, since a child's arm is not long enough to reach the spot, she must toss the ball on one bounce, to the spot where the ball will be hit.

Step 2. She steps in as needed with the front foot and hits the ball.

Step 3. The correct follow-through shows the racket pointed at the opponent. NOTE: Players who hit the backhand with two hands should have enough time, after tossing the ball, to grip the racket with two hands and swing. Also, tell your child to hold the follow-through position momentarily before attempting the next shot. Again, this follow-through is correct for players using an eastern or continental grip.

SERVICE DRILL

Step 1. The best way to practice the serve is to use a ball hopper and try to hit all of the balls into the appropriate service box, using the correct technique. Begin by putting the ball hopper a yard or two to the side so your child won't knock it over with a swing. Standing sideways to the net in the correct serving position, she begins by placing the racket in the back-scratch position.

Step 2. Notice how the toss requires full extension of the arm. A good exercise to demonstrate the point is playing catch. Try to make certain that the ball is released when the arm is fully extended. Tell your child that the service motion is very much like the throwing motion.

Step 3. The follow-through shows the racket pointed toward the ground and to the rear.

USING A BACKBOARD OR WALL

Your child drops and hits a ball against a wall or backboard in the same fashion as if she was on a court, as described in the preceding drills. She must stand far enough from the wall so there is time after the ball comes off the wall and bounces once to swing and hit it a second time. She shouldn't be so far away that the ball will stop bouncing or will have bounced several times before it reaches her. With practice, a child can play the ball off the wall or backboard with increasing consistency. In the beginning, successfully hitting the ball two or three times in a row will deserve much praise. Note: Since the wall area is most likely enclosed, use only one ball. If there are other balls on the ground, your child could trip and fall over the unused and unnecessary balls.

Chapter Seven

KEEPING SCORE AND PLAYING GAMES

When your child can adequately perform the movement drills, he should be encouraged to play actual games even if he is not hitting with much consistency or proficiency. At first, double faults (failing to get either service attempt into the service box) and missed returns of serve (failing to get an opponent's serve back over the net) will be the norm. Keep in mind that it takes a child longer to learn to serve correctly than to hit a forehand or backhand. If a serve can't be hit correctly, your child can serve by dropping and hitting the ball on one bounce with a forehand stroke.

Before beginning a game, your child needs to know basic rules of the game, which follow. A summary of the rules of the United States Tennis Association appears in the Appendix.

SCORING

After a warm-up but before starting to play and keep score, the players decide who serves first and from which side of the court he serves. The traditional method is for one player to "spin the racket" in his hand and the opponent to call "up" or "down." Both players then look to see if the name, letter or symbol at the base of the grip of the racket have landed in an up or a down position. The player who wins the spin chooses to serve or receive, or the side of the court he prefers to begin on. Once the first player makes a choice, the second player selects the remaining option. Conventional scoring, used at tournaments and in most televised matches, can be confusing for a beginner, especially a child. The "No-Ad" scoring system, described below, is recommended because it is extremely easy for you to teach and for your child to learn. The No-Ad scoring system eliminates the deuce-advantage situations of conventional scoring; if the score reaches three points each, the next point decides the game.

Games

In the "No-Ad" scoring system, points are counted 0-1-2-3-4. A point is won in one of two ways: when either player fails to safely return a ball over the net and within the lines of the court, or when a server fails to get either of two balls into the correct service box, in which case a double fault is declared and the point is awarded to the opponent. (Note that the same player serves an entire game.) The first player to win four points wins the game. If the score reaches three points apiece, the receiving player chooses either the left or the right side of the court to receive the deciding serve. No game can possibly have more than seven points.

Sets

Whoever wins six games first wins what is called a *set*, except that he or she must win by two games. If the score is tied at six games apiece, a tie-breaker is played.

The Tie-breaker: There are two types of tie-breakers, a nine-point tie-breaker and a twelve-point tie-breaker. The twelve-point tie-breaker is played in tournaments. The nine-point version is recommended for beginning children because it is much easier to learn: The player whose turn it is to serve the next game is the first server. Call him Player A. He serves the first two points, then Player B serves points three and four. Players change sides of the net after the fourth point. Player A serves points five and six. Player B serves the last three points, if necessary. The first player to win five points wins the tie-breaker.

A doubles tie-breaker is played slightly differently in that Player C (A's partner) serves points five and six, and Player D (B's partner) serves the last three points, if necessary.

Matches

Tournament "matches" for children are normally the best two of three sets. Tournament matches for professionals can be the best three of five sets. I suggest you limit matches to a six-game set for beginning youngsters.

SINGLES PLAY

The first point of every game, whether singles or doubles, begins with the server hitting the ball from behind the base line on the right side of the center mark, across the net and into the diagonally opposite service box.

The second point of every game is played by having the server hit the ball from behind the base line on the left side of the center mark into the diagonally opposite service box. Players alternate left and right positions after each point until the game is over. Players change ends of the court after completion of odd-numbered games (games one, three, five, etc.).

For a thorough description of singles and doubles play see the USTA rules on pages 115-121.

DOUBLES PLAY

Points and games are played in the same fashion in doubles as in singles. With service, either player of the team serving first can elect to serve the first game. Then, either player of the other team can serve the second game. The second player of the first team serves game three and the fourth player serves game four. Once all players have served, service continues in the same manner and order until the set is over. There can be no change of order until the set is completed. Also, once a player receives serve in either the left or right service box, he must continue to receive serve on that side of the court until the set is over. Teams change ends of the court after odd-numbered games, as in singles.

THE "UNWRITTEN" RULES OF PLAY

Tennis is sometimes referred to as a game for ladies and gentlemen. It has also been called a game for blue bloods or royalty. This is, in part, due to its origins as a game only the nobility could play. Such a label, however, no longer applies to the game of tennis in the United States, although it may still be the case in many parts of

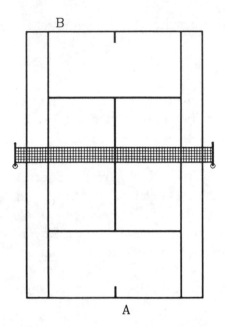

The first, and each alternating, point of every singles game is served from the right side of the court, on the right side of the center mark.

The second, and each alternating, point of every game is served from the left side of the court, on the left side of the service mark.

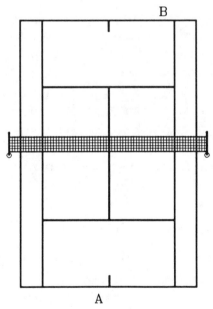

Coaching Tennis

Service in doubles games proceeds just as in singles games. Notice how the serving and receiving players stand at the base line, and their partners stand near the net, which is the customary way doubles is played, but the rules do not require the partners to position themselves that way.

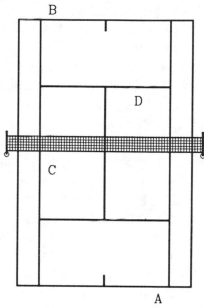

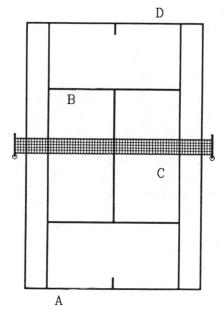

When service alternates to the left side, the opposing team adjusts its position as shown.

the world. In the United States the game is accessible to all players, regardless of any social factors.

Tennis players, however, have played according to an unwritten code of conduct, which is intended for play to be quite genteel and civil. The Code, as it is now known, has been put in writing by Colonel Nick Powell and is available free of charge from the USTA to any member. Nonmembers have to pay a small fee.

The Code of Conduct refers to the informal rules that govern play when there are no linesmen, umpires or referees to settle disputes. You won't find anything in the official rules of the game (Appendix, page 115) that covers the issues found in the Code. In truth, it isn't too much different from friends playing one-on-one basketball and calling their own fouls, but it is a bit more elaborate. The most common problem is calling lines. The rule is that each player calls all balls that land on his side of the court. Even when a player is sure a ball was good, if his opponent calls it out, the point is won by the receiving player. The call is final unless the receiving player changes his mind. This rule applies to serves as well and it is, there-fore, a good idea to play all returns of serve unless the opponent calls the ball out.

Another example of a potential dispute is the double-bounce situation. Player A hits a shot and thinks that Player B didn't hit the ball until the ball had bounced twice. Player B disagrees. In this situation, it is Player B who makes the call. If Player B says he got the ball on one bounce, that is the final decision.

Another example is a player touching the net. If a player hits the net with his racket, or any part of his body touches the net while the ball is still in play, the point is awarded to the opponent. However, it is the player who touches the net who makes the call. Even if Player B is sure that Player A hit the net, unless Player A admits it, Player A doesn't lose the point.

Certainly, hard feelings can result if a player doesn't make the calls fairly, but the game continues under the same unwritten rules until play is concluded. In friendly matches, with nothing at stake but pride, usually no one takes it too seriously. In official tourna-ments, players call the tournament referee if a problem persists.

With beginners, it is important to teach fair play. Without doubt, they will make incredibly bad calls at times, both for and against themselves. Teaching children about sportsmanship, behavior and decorum is an important part of the parent/coach's responsibility.

TEAM PLAY

After your child has learned the basics of how to hit the forehand, backhand, serve, volley and overhead, if not before, he will want to play against other children. League play with teams is a great way for a child to begin competitive play. There are several organizations that sponsor leagues, such as the USTA's National Junior Tennis League or Junior Team Tennis program. If there is no league in your area, ask your local pro if he is willing to start one. To do this, a facility with a number of regularly available courts is needed.

If there are enough interested children and an adequate court situation, a team tennis league can be organized in the following manner:

- Publicize the league and particularly the day for children to sign up or try out.
- On the try-out day, score each child on a 1-to-5 scale, assessing his or her ability to hit the five basic strokes.
- Total all scores and assign players to teams as evenly as possible.
- Based on the number of courts and the number of children, you can structure a format to suit any situation.
- Create a schedule of matches and distribute the schedule to all children and their parents.
- Score each match, record results, and post the league standings.

The rules can be modified to fit the situation. For example, you can allow children to drop and hit a forehand into the service box if it is likely that some children would otherwise commit numerous double faults when serving. Free substitutions can be permitted. If necessary, players could even hit balls on the second bounce.

Once everyone understands the rules, the most important task for the pro or league director is to pair the children so the matches are competitive at the beginning level. Teaching the children how to keep score, where to stand, when to change sides, where to serve, etc., requires both time and patience.

It is recommended that at least one knowledgeable adult or older child work with the children on each court, assisting with the rules and providing encouragement. It is important that the transition from practice to playing matches be an enjoyable experience. As stated throughout this book, if children enjoy playing tennis, they will want to play again. If it is not fun, they simply will not want to participate in future sessions. If done well, the team concept can be less stressful and more fun than individual competition.

TOURNAMENT PLAY

If your child enjoys playing tennis and likes to compete, eventually he will want to play in tournaments. It would be unusual if a child didn't lose in the first round of his first few tournaments. For some, the experience is not enjoyable and they shy away from competition. For others, it's just another new experience.

It is advisable to delay tournament play until your child is ready. Team play and competition with friends can keep your youngster busy. It is also a good idea for your child to watch the early rounds of a tournament before actually entering one.

When you decide that your child is ready to enter a tournament, choose one that is right for him. First of all, look for a tournament close to home, preferably at a park where he has played and is comfortable. Next, look for a tournament that has consolation events for first-round losers. If your child can convince his best friend to enter so they can play doubles together, it is more likely that they will both have fun. Tournament schedules are prepared every year for every part of the country. The USTA is divided into seventeen sections and each has its own publication. A child must be a member of the USTA to play in any sanctioned tournament. Upon joining, he can obtain a tournament schedule by writing directly to the appropriate section. The addresses for the various sections are listed in the Appendix.

Chapter Eight

ACTIVITIES, BOOKS AND VIDEOS

Every aspiring young football or baseball player has a favorite star and a favorite team. Interest is cultivated and developed by articles in newspapers and magazines as well as by playing cards, books and games seen on TV or in person. Once your child shows an interest in tennis, you can nurture it by providing material and information depicting the fun, excitement and glamor of becoming an accomplished tennis player. Listed below are some things to consider.

USTA MEMBERSHIP

Register your child as a member of the USTA. The United States Tennis Association (USTA) is the governing body for tennis in the United States. By joining the USTA, your child automatically becomes a member of one of the seventeen regional associations throughout the country (see page 122). Also, once your child becomes a member, he or she will receive a full year's subscription to *Tennis USTA*, the official monthly newsletter of the USTA, plus a year's subscription to *Tennis Magazine*. This excellent magazine includes pictures of players, instructional articles, tournament results, etc. The USTA also has books and videos for sale. Your child will be put in contact with the entire tennis-playing community, including all local and sectional activities. There are many other benefits to USTA membership, so it is a bargain at this cost. For more information, you may write to the USTA at 70 West Red Oak Lane, White Plains, New York 10604.

USE YOUR LIBRARY

Visit the public library. Autobiographies of some of the great tennis players may be of interest to youngsters. The stories of Arthur Ashe,

Maureen "Little Mo" Connolly, Chris Evert Lloyd, Bjorn Borg and Billie Jean King, just to name a few, should be of inspiration to anyone, regardless of age. There are many instructional books as well for you and your older child. I recommend the following titles:

Autobiographies

Days of Grace: A Memoir, Arthur Ashe and Arnold Rampersad (Alfred A. Knopf, 1993)

Off the Court, Arthur Ashe with Neil Amdur (New American Library, 1981)

Arthur Ashe: Portrait in Motion, Arthur Ashe with Frank Deford (Houghton Mifflin Company, 1975)

Bjorn Borg: My Life and Game, as told to Eugene L. Scott (Simon and Schuster, 1980)

Don Budge: A Tennis Memoir, Don Budge (The Viking Press, 1969)

Power Tennis, Maureen Connolly (A.S. Barnes & Company, 1954)

Court on Court: A Life in Tennis, Margaret Smith Court with George McGann (Dodd, Mead & Company, 1975)

Chrissie: My Own Story, Chris Evert Lloyd with Neil Amdur (Simon and Schuster, 1982)

Lloyd on Lloyd, Chris Evert Lloyd and John Lloyd (Beaufort Books, 1985)

Evonne! On the Move, Evonne Goolagong with Bud Collins (E.P. Dutton Co., Inc., 1975)

Billie Jean King, Billie Jean King with Kim Chapin (Harper & Row, 1974)

Ivan Lendl's Power Tennis, as told to Eugene L. Scott (Simon and Schuster, 1983)

Tennis My Way, Martina Navratilova with Mary Carillo (Charles Scribner's Sons, 1983)

Biographies

The Fireside Book of Tennis: A Complete History of the Game and Its Great Players and Matches, edited by Allison Danzig and Peter Schwed (Simon and Schuster, 1972)

The Goddess and the American Girl: The Story of Suzanne Lenglen and Helen Wills, Larry Engelmann (Oxford University Press, 1988)

Famous Tennis Players, Trent Frayne (Dodd, Mead & Co., 1977)

A Long Way, Baby: Behind the Scenes in Women's Pro Tennis, Grace Lichtenstein (William Morrow & Company, 1974)

Once a Champion: Legendary Tennis Stars Revisited (Dodd, Mead & Company, 1985)

The Lew Hoad Story, by Lew Hoad with Jack Pollard (Prentice-Hall, Inc., 1958)

The Bjorn Borg Story, Jim Tate (Henry Regnery Co., 1974)

Instructional

Tennis for Everyone, Pauline Betz Addie (Acropolis Books Ltd., 1973)

Tennis and Kids: The Family Connection, James Fannin with John Mullin (Doubleday, 1979)

Tennis, Pancho Gonzales and Dick Hawk, edited by Gladys Heldman (Cornerstone Library, 1965)

Tennis to Win, Billie Jean King with Kim Chapin (Harper & Row, 1970)

How to Play Championship Tennis, Rod Laver with Jack Pollard (The Macmillan Company, 1972)

Tennis for Beginners, Bill Murphy and Chet Murphy (Ronald Press Co., 1958)

Tennis for Women, Wendy Overton (Doubleday, 1973)

Tennis for Anyone!, Sarah Palfrey (Hawthorn Books, 1966)

Tennis Tactics: Singles and Doubles, William F. Talbert and Bruce S. Old (Harper & Row, 1983)

Tennis Clinic: Play the Tennis America Way, Dennis Van der Meer (Hawthorn Books, 1974)

Tennis: Myth of the Big Game, Ellsworth Vines and Gene Vier (Viking Press, 1978)

Informational

Hard Courts, John Feinstein (Villard Books, 1991)

Ladies of the Court: Grace and Disgrace on the Women's Tennis

Tour, Michael Mewshaw (Crown Publishers, Inc., 1993)
USTA Publication Catalog (USTA, 70 West Red Oak Lane, White Plains, NY 10604)

SPORTS ILLUSTRATED FOR KIDS

Sports Illustrated for Kids depicts the virtues of athletic achievement in a way that children can relate to. All sports are given the attention they deserve. I particularly like the playing cards developed by *Sports Illustrated for Kids*, which depict athletes from all sports. A child can try to collect the cards of all tennis players and become the fan of one or more stars.

VIDEOS

Check out material available on video. There are numerous instructional videos available. The USTA has a national film library for its members. There are also many commercial products available at your local video store and, perhaps, at your local library. The following are a few of the fifty-plus videos currently on the market:

Instructional and Informative

"Billie Jean King: Tennis Everyone," forty-five minutes of instructions on the fundamentals of tennis
"Martina 1989," explains her conditioning process
"The Winning Edge," John McEnroe, Ivan Lendl, Private Lessons with the Pro
"Complete Tennis From the Pros," Volumes 1, 2, 3 and 4, by Jack Kramer
"Jimmy Connors Tennis" Volumes 1 and 2
"Making It—Junior Tennis in America"
"Play Better Tennis, Vol. 1—The Fundamentals"
"Play Better Tennis, Vol. 2—Advanced Techniques"
"Play Your Best Tennis," Volumes 1 and 2
"The Serve in Tennis"
"Sports Hour: Tennis"
"Superstars of Women's Tennis"
"Teaching Kids Tennis With Nick Bollettieri"

"Tennis by Braden"
"Tennis Equipment"
"Tennis My Way" by Chris Evert Lloyd, three volumes
"Tennis Our Way" by Arthur Ashe, Stan Smith and Vic Braden
"Tennis to Win," Volumes 1 and 2
"Tennis With Stan Smith"
"Tennis Workout to Win—With Virginia Wade"
"Vic Braden's Court Etiquette"
"Vic Braden's Tennis for the Future," Volumes 1, 2 and 3
"Attack With Nick Bollettieri and Andre Agassi" (1990)
"Chris Evert" (1979)
"Competitive Edge" (1988)
"Dr. J—On The Court" (1986)
"Fair Game: Tennis Played by the Rules" (1985)
"Fundamentally Sound Tennis" (1988)
"Game of Control" (1986)
"Go for a Winner" (1976)
"How to Beat a Better Tennis Player" (1983)
"Killer Instinct"
"In Pursuit of #1" (1977)
"Leap to the Top—Applying Plyometrics" (1990), intermediate and
    upper body drills
"Mental Toughness" (1984)
"Mental Toughness—16-Second Cure, With Dr. Jim Loehr" (1988)
"Play It Straight" (1978)
"Smash Hit" (1987)
"Teaching Tennis the USTA Way—Fun and Fundamentals" (1990)
"Tennis Drill Video for Pros and Coaches: Volume I" (1989)
"Tennis Drill Video for Pros and Coaches: Volume II" (1990)
"Tennis Tips Video" (1990)
"Test to Be Your Best: USTA Fitness Testing Protocol" (1990)
"That Special Partnership: Player, Parent, Coach" (1990)

Entertainment
"First Hundred Years" (1981)
"Great Moments in the History of Tennis"

"Greatest Tennis Match of All Time" (1972)
"Laugh and Win"
"New Era" (1973)
"U.S. Open 1977"
"U.S. Open 1988"

Biographical

"Bjorn Borg," thirty minutes of interviews and footage from his career

"Jimmy Connors," thirty minutes of interviews and footage of his career

"Wimbledon Tennis: 1979-80" featuring Borg vs. McEnroe

WATCH TOURNAMENTS AND MATCHES

When you can, and in appropriate doses, watch matches in person and on television. If you are fortunate enough to live in an area where the tour makes a stop, you might be surprised how an in-person look at Steffi Graf, Gabriela Sabatini, Zina Garrison, Jim Courier, Pete Sampras, Andre Agassi, Boris Becker, Stefan Edberg, or any of the other stars might have a great positive effect on your youngster.

PUT A POSTER ON THE WALL

After a while, your child may have a favorite player or star. Get a poster of that player and put it on the bedroom wall.

COLLECT TENNIS CARDS

Your child can have fun collecting tennis cards, as he would collect baseball, basketball or football cards. The Texas-based Tennis Express (P.O. Box 22347, Houston, Texas 77227, 800/833-6615) sells, playing cards of the top male and female players, in addition to a "legends" set.

Tennis card collecting can be a fun
and inspiring hobby for young tennis
players.

Nathalie Tauziat

1 9 9 3 ●WTA

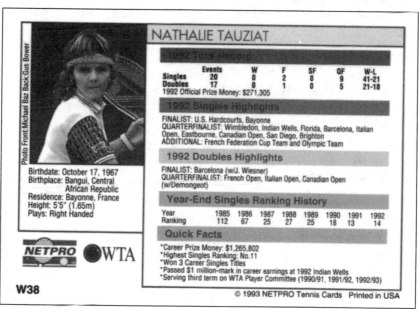

Photo Front:Michael Baz Back:Gus Bower

NATHALIE TAUZIAT

1992 Tour Record

	Events	W	F	SF	QF	W-L
Singles	20	0	2	0	9	41-21
Doubles	17	0	1	0	5	21-18

1992 Official Prize Money: $271,305

1992 Singles Highlights

FINALIST: U.S. Hardcourts, Bayonne
QUARTERFINALIST: Wimbledon, Indian Wells, Florida, Barcelona, Italian
Open, Eastbourne, Canadian Open, San Diego, Brighton
ADDITIONAL: French Federation Cup Team and Olympic Team

1992 Doubles Highlights

FINALIST: Barcelona (w/J. Wiesner)
QUARTERFINALIST: French Open, Italian Open, Canadian Open
(w/Demongeot)

Year-End Singles Ranking History

Year	1985	1986	1987	1988	1989	1990	1991	1992
Ranking	112	67	25	27	25	18	13	14

Quick Facts

*Career Prize Money: $1,265,802
*Highest Singles Ranking: No.11
*Won 3 Career Singles Titles
*Passed $1 million-mark in career earnings at 1992 Indian Wells
*Serving third term on WTA Player Committee (1990/91, 1991/92, 1992/93)

Birthdate: October 17, 1967
Birthplace: Bangui, Central
African Republic
Residence: Bayonne, France
Height: 5'5" (1.65m)
Plays: Right Handed

NETPRO ●WTA

W38

© 1993 NETPRO Tennis Cards   Printed in USA

Chapter Nine

WHEN DOES THE BEGINNING STAGE END?

Depending on the age at which they begin and how regularly they practice and play, it takes children at least a year or two to become skilled enough to be considered an advanced beginner or an intermediate player. Whether a player is a beginner or an intermediate is of little real significance and is difficult to assess objectively. The USTA has prepared a skills test that establishes the categories of beginner, advanced beginner, intermediate, advanced intermediate and advanced players. They also provide certificates, badges and testing kits that help children enjoy their success a little more and give them specific goals to aim for. You may obtain the materials at little cost by writing to the USTA, 70 West Red Oak Lane, White Plains, New York 10604.

In my opinion, a beginning player can be considered an intermediate player when he or she can play matches with sustained rallies, while keeping score and knowing the rules of play and etiquette. Match strategy and how to hit strokes such as drop shots, lobs, approach shots, etc., are topics for the intermediate player. Children who truly like playing the game of tennis will play because they want to play and not because they want to become an intermediate or advanced player. As long as your child is having fun and executing the fundamentals correctly, he will continue to improve with virtually no limit to how good he can become.

By the time your child becomes an intermediate player, if not before, you should be playing games with your child, as I urge all nonplaying parents to do. You can begin to enjoy the experience from an entirely different perspective as you learn and grow as a tennis player along with your child. Do the best you can to make certain that your child is learning correctly. More important, have fun with your child so you both will want to continue playing together. Don't be in a hurry to get to the next level. The beginning stage can be a wonderful time for you and your child. Your child won't be little for long and he will never be little again. The relationship you establish with your child on a tennis court may very well set the tone for your future relationship. Do a good job and you may experience a lifetime of shared fun, because tennis truly is a game for a lifetime.

Future hopefuls.

GLOSSARY

Ace: A shot hit into the proper service box that the opponent is unable to touch.

Alley: The area between the singles lines and the doubles lines.

Backcourt: The area between the service line and the base line.

Backhand: A shot hit by a right-handed player on the left side of his body, or, for a left-handed player, a ball hit on the right side of his body.

Backswing: That portion of the swing when a player brings his racket back to prepare to hit a shot.

Base line: The line running parallel to the net, at the back of the court on each side of the net.

Butt: The bottom portion of a racket frame. A symbol or letter indicating the name of the manufacturer is usually imprinted on the butt of the racket.

Center line: The line that divides the left-hand service box from the right-hand service box.

Center mark: The mark on the base line that divides the court in half and lines up with the center line.

Changeover: The time when players change ends of the court after odd games.

Closed racket face: A racket face angled down toward the ground.

Continental grip: One of the three general categories of grips. With the continental grip, no change of hand position on the racket is required in order to hit any shot.

Court surface: Tennis courts are categorized by the type of surface used to construct the court: hard court, clay court, grass court or wooden surface (such as a gymnasium floor).

Deuce: In conventional scoring, the score when the points are tied in any game at 40 apiece.

Double fault: Failing to serve a ball in the proper court after two attempts; the point is awarded to the receiver.

Doubles: A match with two players on each team.

Doubles lines: The outside lines of the court that run perpendicular to the net.

Eastern grip: The orthodox method of holding a racket, at least in the United States. Players who use this grip must change grips to hit the forehand, backhand and other shots.

Error: Missing a shot or not getting the ball in the court or over the net. An error can be an unforced error or a forced error depending on how difficult the shot was for the player to hit.

Face: The stringed portion of the racket.

Flat serve (flat shot): A shot hit without any spin on the ball.

Follow-through: The way a player finishes a swing, after contact is made and the ball has left the racket.

Footwork: The way a player moves his feet to get into position in order to hit a shot.

Forehand: A shot hit by a right-handed player on the right side of his body, or, for a left-handed player, a shot hit on the left side.

Frame: The entire racket except the strings.

Front court: The area of the court between the net and the service line.

Game: When players compete against each other, they attempt to win points. When a player wins enough points, he wins a game.

Grip: The way a player holds a racket. Also, the leather portion of the racket handle. The size of a grip may vary from racket to racket. The size of a player's hand determines what size grip is best for the player.

Ground strokes: A forehand or backhand shot, as distinguished from a serve, volley, overhead or other stroke.

Half volley: A ball hit on a short hop.

Head: The top portion of the racket frame or the top of the stringed portion of the racket.

Let: The call when a ball from another court interrupts play, or some other distraction occurs; the point is replayed.

Let cord: The call when a ball hits the top of the net and goes over. When a let cord occurs on a serve, the server is given another opportunity to hit the ball, provided the ball landed in the service box after hitting the net. When the ball hits the net and goes over on any shot other than the serve, play continues without interruption.

Lob: A ball lofted high in the air; it can be an offensive shot or a defensive shot.

Match: When players or teams compete against each other, they are said to be playing a "match" against one another. Most matches require winning two of three sets.

Midcourt: The middle area of the court in the vicinity of the service lines.

Neck: The throat area of a racket.

Net: The net divides the court in half. It is usually made of rope-like netting but sometimes is a metal or wirelike material.

Net posts: The poles to which the net is attached.

No-man's-land: The area between the service line and the base line. It is said that a player should not be caught standing in this area because he or she is vulnerable to a variety of shots and is therefore at a tactical disadvantage.

Open face: A racket angled up, toward the sky.

Out: A ball landing outside the lined area of the court. Balls that hit the lines are good.

Overhead: A ball that is over a player's head, hit by the player in a servicelike motion. A player usually hits an overhead after his opponent hits a lob.

Passing shot: A ball hit past an opponent when that opponent is at the net.

Point: Once a server attempts to get a ball into the court to begin a game, someone will win the point. Players compete for points in order to win games.

Rally: Hitting a ball back and forth between players, whether in practice or in a match.

Ready position: The position a player stands in while awaiting the opponent's shot.

Semiwestern grip: An increasingly popular grip used on an advanced level for generating spin and power, but not for volleys or serves. This grip requires a hand change to hit a backhand.

Serve: The shot that a player hits to begin a point.

Service box: The area into which a player must hit the ball to begin a point. There is a right-hand service box and a left-hand service box on each side of the net.

Service break: Loss of the game by the server.

Service line: The line running parallel to the net, approximately halfway between the net and the base line.

Set: In the conventional scoring system, as used in tournaments, the first player who wins six games wins a set.

Sidelines: *see* **doubles lines**.

Strings: The material used inside the top portion of the racket frame. In years past, strings were either nylon or "catgut." Now strings are made of synthetic gut and nylon.

Throat: The portion of the racket between the handle of the racket and the racket head.

Volley: Hitting a ball in the air without letting the ball hit the ground first (unless the ball is hit in a servicelike motion, in which case it is an overhead stroke).

Western grip: One of the three most common methods of holding a racket, together with the eastern grip and the continental grip.

Winner: A shot hit into an opponent's court that is out of the reach of the opponent.

DIAGRAM OF COURT

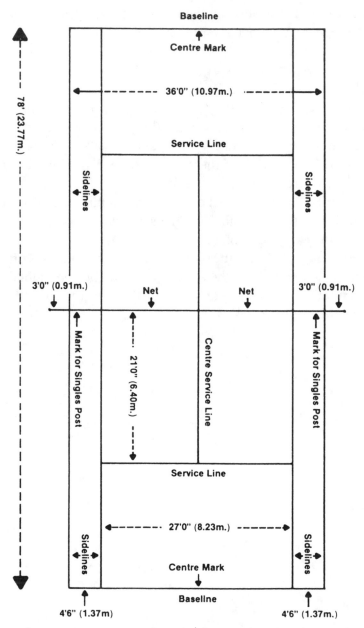

All measurements are made to the outside edge of the lines.

SUMMARIZED RULES OF TENNIS

The following is reprinted by permission of the United States Tennis Association.

Introduction

The official rules of tennis are summarized below for the convenience of all players. In the preparation of this summary, no changes were made in the official rules, which have been established by the International Tennis Federation and are adhered to by the United States Tennis Association. Some technical aspects, however, such as specifications on court size and equipment, balls and rackets, have been deleted here for the sake of brevity. For those who are interested in these specifications, they are covered in their entirety in the complete Rules of Tennis, which also includes interpretative Cases and Decisions and USTA Comments.

Another invaluable reference for players is the Code, whose principles and guidelines apply to unofficiated matches (see page 98). Players all over the world follow not only the official rules of tennis but also the traditions of sportsmanship and fair play found in the Code.

A familiarity with these rules and traditions is essential for achieving the greatest possible benefit and enjoyment from tennis.

The Singles Game

Server and Receiver: The players stand on opposite sides of the net; the player who first delivers the ball is called the server and the other the receiver.

Choice of Sides and Service: The choice of ends and the right to be server or receiver in the first game is decided by toss. The player winning the toss may choose or require his opponent to choose: (a) the right to be server or receiver, in which case the other player shall choose the end; or (b) the end, in which case the other player shall choose the right to be server or receiver.

Delivery of Service: The service is delivered in the following manner. Immediately before commencing to serve, the server shall stand with both feet at rest behind the base line and within the imaginary continuations of the center mark and the sideline. He shall not serve until the receiver is ready.

The server then throws the ball into the air in any direction and strikes it with his racket before it hits the ground. Delivery is deemed complete at the moment the racket strikes the ball.

Return of Service: The receiver may stand wherever he pleases on his own side of the net. However, he must allow the ball to hit the ground in the service court before returning it. If the receiver attempts to return the service, he shall be deemed ready.

Service From Alternate Courts: In delivering the service, the server stands alternately behind the right and left courts, beginning from the right in every game. The ball served shall pass over the net and hit the ground within the service court which is diagonally opposite, or upon any line bounding such court, before the receiver returns it.

If the ball is erroneously served from the wrong half of the court, the resulting play stands, but service from the proper court, in accordance with the score, shall be resumed immediately after this discovery.

Faults: The service is a fault if the server misses the ball in attempting to serve it, if the ball does not land in the proper service court, or if the ball served touches a permanent fixture other than the net, strap or band before it hits the ground.

Throughout the delivery of the service, the server shall not change his position by walking or running. A foot fault is called when the server touches the base line or the imaginary continuation of either the sideline or the center line while he is in the process of serving. However, having his foot in the air over one of these lines is not a foot fault.

Service After a Fault: After a fault (if it is the first fault) the server serves again from behind the same half of the court from which he served that fault. If the service was a fault because it was served from behind the wrong half, the server is entitled to deliver one service from behind the proper half of the court.

A Service Let: During the service, a ball that touches the net but lands in the proper court is termed a *let* and counts for nothing. That one service is replayed. There is no limit to the number of let balls that may be made on the service; the server continues serving into the same court until a good service is delivered or two faults are made.

Receiver Becomes Server: At the end of the first game, the receiver becomes server and the server, receiver; and so on alternately in all the subsequent games of a match. The players change ends at the end of the first, third, and every subsequent alternate game of each set, and at the end of each set unless the total number of games in the set is even, in which case the change is not made until the end of the first game of the next set.

If a player serves out of turn, the player who ought to have served shall serve as soon as the mistake is discovered. All points scored before such discovery shall stand. If a game has been completed before such discovery, the order of service remains as altered.

Server Wins Point: The server wins the point if the ball served, not being a let, touches the receiver or anything which he wears or carries before it hits the ground, or if the receiver otherwise loses the point as described below.

Receiver Wins Point: The receiver wins the point if the server serves two consecutive faults, or otherwise loses the point as described below.

Player Loses Point: A player loses the point if:

(a) he fails to return the ball directly over the net before it has hit the ground twice consecutively; or

(b) he returns the ball in play so that it hits the ground, a permanent fixture (other than the net, posts or singles sticks, cord or metal cable, strap or band) or other object outside any of the lines that bound his opponent's court; or

(c) he volleys the ball and fails to make a good return even when standing outside the court; or

(d) he deliberately carries or catches the ball in play on his racket or deliberately touches it with his racket more than once; or

(e) he or his racket touches the net, post or the ground within his opponent's court at any time while the ball is in play; or

(f) he volleys the ball before it has passed the net; or

(g) the ball in play touches him or anything that he wears or carries other than the racket in his hand; or

(h) he throws his racket at and hits the ball; or

(i) he deliberately and materially changes the shape of his racket during the playing of the point; or

(j) he deliberately commits any act which hinders his opponent in making a stroke.

A Good Return: It is a good return if:

(a) the ball touches the net, posts, singles sticks, cord or metal cable, strap or band provided that it passes over any of them and hits the ground within the court; or

(b) the ball, served or returned, hits the ground within the proper court and rebounds or is blown back over the net, and the player whose turn it is to strike reaches over the net and plays the ball, provided that neither he nor any part of his clothes or racket touches the net, posts, singles sticks, cord or metal cable, strap or band or the ground within his opponent's court, and that the stroke is otherwise good; or

(c) the ball is returned outside the posts, or singles sticks, either above or below the level of the top of the net, even though it touches the posts or singles sticks, provided that it hits the ground within the proper court; or

(d) a player's racket passes over the net after he has returned the ball, provided the ball passes the net before being played and is properly returned; or

(e) a player succeeds in returning the ball, served or in play, that strikes another ball lying in the court; or

(f) the ball touches any other permanent fixture after it has hit the ground within the proper court.

Ball Falling on Line—Good: A ball falling on a line is regarded as falling in the court bounded by that line.

A Let: In all cases where a let (other than a service let) has to be called under the rules, or to provide for an interruption of play, the point shall be replayed.

If a player is hindered in making a stroke by anything not within his control, except a permanent fixture or deliberate interference by his opponent, a let shall be called.

Coaching: A player may not receive coaching during the playing of any match other than one that is part of a team competition.

The Doubles Game

The above rules apply to the doubles game except as below.

Delivery of Service: The server positions himself with both feet at least behind the base line and within the imaginary continuations of the center mark and the sideline of the doubles court.

Order of Service: At the beginning of each set, the pair serving the first game decides which partner shall do so and the opposing pair decide similarly for the second game. The partner of the player who served in the first game serves in the third; the partner of the player who served in the second game serves in the fourth, and so on in the same order in all subsequent games of a set.

Order of Receiving: The pair receiving the service in the first game of each set decides which partner shall receive in the right-hand court, and the opposing pair decides similarly in the second game of each set. Partners receive the service alternately throughout each game. The order of receiving the service shall not be altered during the set but may be changed at the beginning of a new set.

Service out of Turn: If a partner serves out of his turn, the partner who ought to have served shall serve as soon as the mistake is discovered, but all points scored and any faults served before such discovery shall stand. If a game has been completed before such discovery, the order of service remains as altered.

Receiving out of Turn: If during a game the order of receiving the service is changed by the receivers, it remains as altered until the end of the game, but the partners shall resume their original order of receiving in the next game of that set in which they are the receivers.

Served Ball Touching Player: The service is a fault if the ball touches the server's partner or anything that he wears or carries. The server wins the point if the ball served (not being a let) touches the partner of the receiver, or anything he wears or carries, before it hits the ground.

Ball Struck Alternately: The ball shall be struck by one or the other player of the opposing pairs in the course of making a serve or a return. If both of them hit the ball, either simultaneously or consecutively, their opponents win the point.

Scoring

A Game: If a player wins his first point, the score is called 15 for that player; on winning his second point, his score is called 30; on winning his third point, his score is called 40; and the fourth point won by a player is scored a game for that player except as follows:

If both players have won three points, the score is called deuce; the next point won by a player is scored advantage for that player. If the same player wins the next point, he wins the game. If the other player wins the next point, the score is again called deuce; and so on until a player wins the two points immediately following the score at deuce, when the game is scored for that player.

A Set: A player (or players) who first wins six games wins a set, except that he must win by a margin of two games over his opponent. Where necessary, a set is extended until this margin is achieved (unless a tie-break system of scoring has been announced in advance of the match).

The maximum of sets in a match is five for men and three for women.

The Tie-Break Game: If announced in advance of the match, a tie-break game operates when the score reaches six games all in any set.

In singles, the player who first wins seven points wins the game and the set provided he leads by a margin of two points. If the score reaches six points all the game is extended until this margin has been achieved. Numerical scoring is used throughout the tie-break. The player whose turn it is to serve is the server for the first point; his opponent is the server for the second and third points; and, thereafter, each player serves alternately for two consecutive points until the winner of the game and set has been decided.

In doubles, the player whose turn it is to serve is the server for the first point. Thereafter, each player serves in rotation for two points, in the same order as determined previously in that set, until the winners of the game and set have been decided.

From the first point, each service is delivered alternately from the right and left courts, beginning from the right court. The first server serves the first point from the right court; the second server serves the second and third points from the left and right courts, respectively; the next server serves the fourth and fifth points from the left and right courts, respectively; and so on.

Players change ends after every six points and at the conclusion of the tie-break game. The player (or doubles pair) who served first in the tie-break shall receive service in the first game of the following set.

Copyright 1983 by the United States Tennis Association
Revised 1988

USTA REGIONAL ASSOCIATIONS

Caribbean Tennis Association
  P.O. Box 40439
  Minillas Station
  Santurce, PR 00940 (809/765-3182)
Eastern Tennis Associaton
  Doris Herrick
  550 Mamaroneck Avenue, Suite 505
  Harrison, NY 10528 (914/698-0414)
Florida Tennis Association
  1280 SW Thirty-Sixth Avenue, Suite 305
  Pompano Beach, FL 33069 (305/968-3434)
Hawaii Tennis Association
  2615 S. King Street, Suite 2A
  Honolulu, HI 96826 (808/955-6696)
Intermountain Tennis Association
  1201 South Parker Road, #200
  Denver, CO 80231 (303/695-4117)
Mid-Atlantic Tennis Association
  2230 George C. Marshall Drive, Suite E
  Falls Church, VA 22043-2582 (703/560-9480)
Middle States Tennis Association
  460 Glennie Circle
  King of Prussia, PA 19406 (610/277-4040)
Missouri Valley Tennis Association
  801 Walnut Street, Suite 100
  Kansas City, MO 64106 (816/472-6882)
USTA/New England Tennis Association
  P.O. Box 587
  Needham Heights, MA 02194 (617/964-2030)
Northern California Tennis Association
  1350 South Loop Road, Suite 100
  Alameda, CA 94502 (510/748-7373)
Northwestern Tennis Association
  5525 Cedar Lake Road
  St. Louis Park, MN 55416 (612/546-0709)

USTA/Pacific Northwest Tennis Association
    4840 SW Western Avenue, Suite 300
    Beavertown, OR 97005-3430 (503/520-1877)
Southern California Tennis Association
    Robert Kramer
    P.O. Box 240015
    Los Angeles, CA 90024-9115 (310/208-3838)
Southern Tennis Association
    3850 Holcomb Bridge Road, Suite 305
    Norcross, GA 30092 (404/368-8200)
Southwestern Tennis Association
    6330 East Thomas Road, Suite 2-120
    Scottsdale, AZ 85251-7055 (602/947-9293)
Texas Tennis Association
    Executive Director Ken McAllister
    2111 Dickson, Suite 33
    Austin, TX 78704 (512/443-1334)
Western Tennis Association
    Kay Schubert
    8720 Castle Creek Parkway, Suite 329
    Indianapolis, IN 46250 (317/577-5130)
USTA
    Corporate Offices
    70 West Red Oak Lane
    White Plains, NY 10604 (914/696-7000)

RACKET MANUFACTURERS

There are more than twenty-five manufacturers of tennis rackets in the United States. Not all of them make rackets for children. The following is a list of most, if not all, manufacturers who market rackets for children.

DUNLOP
P.O. Box 3070
Greenville, SC 29602
(800) 476-5400

HEAD
4801 North Sixty-Third Street
Boulder, CO 80301
(800) 257-5100

NASSAU
95 Blackburn Center
Gloucester, MA 01930
(800) 255-7812

PRINCE
P.O. Box 2031
Princeton, NJ 08540
(800) 2-TENNIS

PRO-KENNEX
9606 Kearney Villa Road
San Diego, CA 92126
(800) 854-1908

ROSSIGNOL
115 Court Street
Exeter, NH 03833

WILSON
2233 West Street
River Grove, IL 60171

WIMBLEDON/TIME SPORTS
P.O. Box 9418
Trenton, NJ 08650
(800) 446-5683

YONEX
3520 Challenger Street
Torrance, CA 90503
(800) 44 YONEX

ZEBEST
P.O. Box 71
Alpharetta, GA 30201
(800) 272-7279

JUNIOR RACKETS

The following is a sampling of the alternatives available. At the low end of the price range are the aluminum rackets, starting as low as twenty-five dollars. High-end rackets are graphite and fiberglass composition types, with prices up to about seventy-five dollars.

Wilson Sporting Goods Co. offers six junior rackets. The Jr. Widebody 23 is 23 inches long and made of aluminum. It has a 3⅞-inch grip size and a 90-square-inch racket head.

The Jr. Widebody 25 is also made of aluminum and is 25 inches long. The racket face is 90 square inches and the grip is 4 inches.

The Jr. Advantage 110 is also made of aluminum and comes with a 110-square-inch head. There is a smaller 95-square-inch version as well. The grip is 4 inches.

The Rack Attack is made of a 15 percent graphite composition and has a 95-square-inch head. It comes with a 4-inch grip.

The Junior Profile is made of 30 percent graphite composition with a 95-square-inch racket face and a 4-inch grip.

Prince Manufacturing Co. has two collections of rackets for junior players. The J/R Series consists of three aluminum rackets of three lengths—21 inches (J/R Mini); 23½ inches (J/R Tour); and 25½ inches (J/R Pro). The racket face of each is 90 square inches. The grip size for the 21-inch mini model is 3⅝ inches. For the 23½-inch J/R Tour the grip size is 3¾-inches. For the J/R Pro the grip size is 4 inches.

The other junior rackets offered by Prince are called the Ace Face Collection. It consists of two rackets. The smallest racket in the line is the J/R Ace Face, which is 25½ inches long, made of aluminum with a 4-inch grip. It comes with either a 90-square-inch racket face or a 110-square-inch face. It is very much like the J/R Pro but a bit heavier.

The Ace Face is 27 inches long and is made of graphite and fiberglass. The racket face can be either 90 square inches or 110 square inches. The grip comes in sizes varying from 4 to 4½ inches.

INDEX

Lines
   calling, 98
   running, 67
Lines, court, 15-17
   base, 110
   center, 110
   diagram, 16-17, 114
   doubles, 110
   stance, 20-21
Lob, 64, 111

M

Manufacturers, racket, 124
Match, 94-95, 112
Mid-Atlantic Tennis Association, 122
Middle States Tennis Association, 122
Missouri Valley Tennis Association, 122

N

Nassau rackets, 124
Net, touching, 98
Northern California Tennis Association, 122
Northwestern Tennis Association, 122

O

Overhead. *See* Stroke, overhead

P

Play
   league, 99
   team, 99-100
   tournament, 100
Points, winning, 94
   See also Service, points
Practice
   backboard or wall, 92
   ball machine, 87
   ball throwing, 72-73
   program, 67

   sessions, 13, 66-92
Practice drills
   backhand, 90
   circle hit, 76
   combination, 76
   crossover feed-in, 80
   diagrams 68-71
   forehand, 89
   four-position, 75
   hitting, 68-71
   movement, 74-81
   shadow, 75
   side-to-side, 78
   three-position, 74
   two-position, 74
   up-and-back, 77
   windshield wipers, 79
Practice games, 82-83
   baseball (catching), 84
   baseball (hitting), 83
   baseball (pitching), 83-84
   basketball (dribbling), 85
   basketball (horse), 85
   basketball (lay-up drill), 85
   elimination, 82
   mini-tennis, 82
   most balls bounced off the racket, 82
   most balls dropped and hit over the net, 82
   most balls hit over the net, 82
   most serves hit into the correct service box, 82
   name that line, 85
   running lines, 88
   running races, 84-85
   shuttle run, 88
Prince rackets, 124-125
Pro-Kennex rackets, 124